CONSTANTINE COLLE
COLLEGE LIBRARY SERVICE

Books should be returned on or before the last date stamped below

HFS

25. SEP. 1970

-8 JAN. 1971

23. APR. 1971

-7. MAY 1971

11. JUN. 1971

27. OCT. 1972

2. FEB. 1973

20. JUN.

WHINCUP, M. H   16760

To renew this book return it for restamping or quote the above details in writing or by telephone. FINES ARE CHARGED FOR OVERDUE BOOKS

LIB/PF/5

THE SUPERVISOR'S BOOKSHELF

General Editor: J. J. HENDERSON
Director, Institute of Supervisory Management

Industrial Law

Industrial Law

MICHAEL H. WHINCUP, LL.M.
Barrister-at-Law
Lecturer in Law at the University of Keele

Published in association with the
INSTITUTE OF SUPERVISORY MANAGEMENT

HEINEMANN : LONDON

William Heinemann Ltd
LONDON   MELBOURNE   TORONTO
CAPE TOWN   AUCKLAND

© Michael H. Whincup 1968
First published 1968
434 92240 4 (hardback)
434 92241 2 (limp)

Printed in Great Britain by
Cox & Wyman Ltd, London, Fakenham and Reading

To my parents

Foreword

Greater recognition is being given to the job of the supervisor in industry, commerce, and the public service. His contribution to organizational efficiency and employee relations depends on how closely he is integrated into the management he serves. This, in turn, often depends on the skill and knowledge he displays in his work. Whilst company education and training schemes can help enormously in the development of talent, a lot depends on how much initiative the supervisor takes to equip himself for the tasks involved in his managerial role.

The purpose of this series of books on various aspects of management at the supervisory level is to give the go-ahead, alert minded supervisor a start in the right direction. No one can become a first-class supervisor by reading one or several books. The right personal qualities developed through a soundly based training scheme and directly linked to practical experience are essential. But this does not invalidate the point that a well-devised comprehensive series of educational books for supervisors can deepen and broaden their insight into supervisory management responsibilities and equip them to learn more quickly and thoroughly from experience.

The series, called *The Supervisor's Bookshelf*, provides (i) a comprehensive cover of essential subjects, (ii) supporting material for group discussions in I.S.M. local sections and company supervisors' associations, and (iii) additional texts for students reading for the examinations in Supervisory Studies. Each book has been specially commissioned and the individual authors are men with considerable experience of the work, the education and training, and the aspirations of supervisors.

Birmingham   J. J. HENDERSON

The Institute of Supervisory Management

The Institute is a national body whose aim is to promote the appreciation of supervisory management as a profession through education, association, and research. It is concerned to establish and maintain the highest standards of qualification and performance. Membership services include local activities, publications, advice and information, appointments, courses, and conferences. The Institute of Supervisory Management is a self-supporting, voluntary association governed by a Council elected from its members. It is non-political and does not act as a negotiating body upon the question of salaries and wages.

Preface

This book is concerned with the employee's legal rights to security and safety of employment, and with his corresponding duties to fulfil his contract of employment. It is, in other words, concerned with the personal relationship of employer and employee, and not with the organizational problems of management and labour.

I believe that this is an increasingly interesting and important area of law. After years of inactivity considerable changes are now taking place, expressing the growing power and independence of labour. Recent Acts of Parliament have introduced minimum periods of notice and redundancy benefits, and given greater protection to office and shop workers. More rigorous safety requirements for many industrial processes have been laid down by statutory instruments. Leading cases have been decided which answer more clearly controversial questions such as the standards of work and integrity which may be expected of employees, and the liability for accidents caused by employees' own indifference to safety precautions. By studying the law's more or less impartial solutions to these common issues of industrial conflict, a greater understanding of the problems of both sides should be gained.

Since the law's value can be measured only by its practical results, I have on occasion stepped outside the conventional confines of a textbook on law, and considered critically some of the more doubtful aspects of the law's operation – particularly as regards awards of damages for injuries at work. I hope in this way to have made this book both informative and stimulating.

I extend grateful thanks to my secretary, Miss Freda Mainwaring, for her willing and careful work on the manuscript.

M. H. W.

Contents

Foreword   v
Preface   vii

1. The Contract of Employment   1

INTRODUCTION   1
Sources of law   1
Purposes of cases cited   2
THE PARTIES TO THE CONTRACT   2
Test of control   3
Division of liability   5
Hiring-out; general and particular employment   5
Apprentices   6
THE FORM OF THE CONTRACT   6
General rule as to written contracts   6
    The Contracts of Employment Act
Collective agreements   8
THE TERMS OF THE CONTRACT   8
Works' rules books   8
Changing the terms   9
Express and implied terms   9
Employer's implied obligations   10
    Safety – Provision of work – Payment – Indemnity – Sick pay – Restraint of trade terms – References
Employee's implied obligations   14
    Obedience – Competence – Care – Good faith
ENDING THE CONTRACT   18
Employee's breach of contract   19
    Strikes

INDUSTRIAL LAW

Employer's breach of contract 21
Wrongful dismissal
Fulfilling the contract 22
Notice
The Redundancy Payments Act 25
Dismissal – Proof of redundancy – Benefits – Disqualifications – Industrial tribunals – Redundancy Fund and rebates
Unemployment insurance 30

2. The Employer's Common Law Liabilities for Safety 32

THE EMPLOYER'S DUTY TO HIS EMPLOYEES 32

Reasonable care 32
Test of reasonableness – Assessment of liability – Employer's personal responsibility
Safe premises 36
Complaints – Maintenance – Working away
Safe equipment 39
General trade practice – Hidden defects – Research and testing
Safe fellow-employees and competent supervision 42
Training – Dangerous employees
Safe system of work 44
Lifting and similar injuries – Inadequate instruction or equipment – Piecework – Liability where employee ignores safety precautions – General safety rules

THE EMPLOYER'S LIABILITIES FOR HIS EMPLOYEES' WRONGFUL ACTS 51

Vicarious liability 51
Liability of wrongdoer – Course of employment – Distinction between contract and course of employment – Financial loss
Liability for independent contractors 57

3. The Employer's Statutory Liabilities for Safety, Health, and Welfare 59

THE FACTORIES ACT, 1961, REGULATIONS FOR DANGEROUS TRADES, AND OTHER OCCUPATIONAL STATUTES 59

Types of employment protected – Regulations on dangerous

xii

CONTENTS

trades – Differences between Acts and common law – Definition of factory – 'Manual labour' – Other processes within the Act – Definitions of mines, offices, etc.

Part I: Health   64
Cleanliness – Overcrowding – Temperature – Ventilation – Lighting – Drainage – Toilets – Enforcement – Medical supervision

Part II: Safety   67
Guarding dangerous machinery – Other rules – Work on unfenced machinery – Sale or hire of machinery – Work by young or unskilled persons – Lifting equipment – Safe place of work – Safe means of access – Dangerous fumes, etc. – Boilers – Fire precautions – Joint safety councils?

Part III: Welfare   79
Drinking and washing facilities – Clothing accommodation – Seats – First aid – Welfare regulations; protective clothing – Safety clothing

Part IV: Health, safety, and welfare (special provisions)   82
Dust and fumes – Meals in dangerous trades – Goggles and screens – Health hazards – Regulations on dangerous trades

Part V: Notification and investigation of accidents and industrial diseases   85
Notifiable accidents – Dangerous occurrences

Part VI: Employment of women and young persons   87
Hours of work – Overtime – Shift work – Miscellaneous exceptions – Medical supervision

Part VII: Special applications and extensions   90

Part VIII: Home work   90

Part IX: Wages   91

Part X: Notices, records, etc.; duties of persons employed   93
Prescribed abstract – General register; periodical returns – Employees' duties – Checkweighing

Part XI: Administration   93

Part XII: Offences, penalties, and legal proceedings 94
Employers' criminal liability – Fines

Part XIII: Application 96

Part XIV: Interpretation and general 96

THE OCCUPIERS' LIABILITY ACT 96
Duty to Visitors 97
Traps – Contractors – Trespassers and children

Owner's liability for equipment 99

4. The Employer's Defences; Damages and Industrial Injuries Insurance 101

Burden of proof 101

DEFENCES 102

Reasonable care 102
Act of God 102
Remoteness of damage 102
Delegation 103
At common law – By statute
Contributory negligence 104
Fault – Motives – Contributory negligence in breach of statutory duty cases
Consent 109
Danger money

DAMAGES 110

General and special damages 110
Basis of assessment – Expectation of life – Damages on death – Time limits
Problems 113
Costs; legal aid and advice – Delay – Compulsory insurance? – Periodic payments? – Absolute liability – Objections

INDUSTRIAL INJURIES INSURANCE BENEFITS 118

National Insurance Acts 118

CONTENTS

Entitlement to benefit 118
Accidents at work – Prescribed diseases
Basic benefits 120
Injury benefit – Disablement benefit – Additional benefits – Disqualification – Death benefit – Claims – Damages and insurance payments

Index 124

1: The Contract of Employment

Introduction
This book outlines the law governing employer and employee in their daily dealings with each other. Much of the law here concerns safety responsibilities, but there are also the problems of security of employment – rules as to standards of work, notice and dismissal without notice, redundancy benefit, and the like. That branch of the law affecting management and labour organizations as such is dealt with in this series in the book entitled *Industrial Relations*, by J. E. Mortimer.

SOURCES OF LAW
There are two main sources of English law, and each provides some of the rules we shall be considering. They are (i) **the common law,** and (ii) **statute law.** The common law consists of important judgments or *precedents* given by our judges and followed by other judges in subsequent similar cases. These rulings involve statements of legal principles devised by the judges themselves. It must be remembered, however, that the application of the rules depends very much on the facts of each particular case. (The purpose of the many cases cited in this book is explained below.) Statute law, on the other hand, is made by Parliament. It includes not only the familiar *Acts of Parliament*, but also rules made by Ministers under powers given to them by these Acts, such as the Power Presses Regulations made by the Minister of Labour under the authority of the Factories Act. These rules are called *statutory instruments* and they represent a large part of the law relating to safety and welfare in factories. Either type of law, or both, may govern any particular industrial problem. The common law rules about employment tend to provide general standards of behaviour which apply wherever one works – whether in a factory or on a farm or elsewhere – whilst Parliament tries to devise more detailed rules for specific kinds of work.

The distinction between common law and statute is not the same as that between civil law and criminal. While most crimes are defined and punishable by Act of Parliament, none the less many Acts create purely civil rights and duties. Nearly all the rules we shall examine are from the civil law, whose main purpose is to compensate the victim of misfortune, rather than to punish the wrongdoer.

PURPOSE OF CASES CITED

Many of the common law rules stated in these chapters are supported by the names of High Court or appeal cases where these propositions can be found. Most of these cases are simply illustrations of the basic principles involved, but their names are given as points of reference for any more detailed enquiry into a particular problem. The judgments may be found in full in one or other of the periodic law reports, such as the *All England Law Reports* or the *Weekly Law Reports*, or they may be referred to more briefly in the *Current Law* series. Details may also be given in other textbooks such as Mansfield-Cooper's *Outlines of Industrial Law* or Munkman's *Employers' Liability*. A very useful work containing a brief account of many of the cases is Bingham's *All the Modern Cases of Negligence*. Others are drawn from *The Times* or other newspapers' law reports, and there are also some Scottish and Commonwealth cases by way of comparison or explanation.

The Parties to the Contract

The relationship of employer and employee (or master and servant as the law still sometimes calls them) is one of the closest known to the law. It carries with it a mass of rights and duties which may not apply at all in other working relationships, e.g. where work is done by a self-employed person. Some of these responsibilities, particularly with regard to safety, have been established in the law for many years. Other rights, more concerned with security, have been more recently created by Act of Parliament. Thus the Contracts of Employment Act, 1963, lays down minimum periods of notice and requirements as to written particulars of employment which do not affect workers other than employees. Again, National Insurance benefits (for unemployment, sickness, industrial injury, etc.) are paid for in part by the contributions of employers and employees. The self-employed pay at different rates and are not eligible for all the benefits. Other Acts require many employers to take on a quota of disabled persons. Newer legislation has tended increasingly to impose financial burdens upon employers, e.g. under the Industrial Training Act, 1964, the Redundancy Payments Act, 1965, and still more recently under the rules of the selective employment tax. Reference is made below to the effects of evading these liabilities.

TEST OF CONTROL

For these various reasons it has become more and more important to distinguish the contract of employment from other contracts for work or services. The difference does not depend merely on payment or the giving of instructions or the stamping of insurance cards. **The vital consideration in deciding whether there is a contract of employment is the degree of control exercised by one man over another.** This is usually expressed as the 'what to do and how to do it' test. If A can tell B not only what job he shall do but also the way in which he shall do it, then the relationship of employer and employee exists. But if A can only tell B what job to do, and how he does it is left to his discretion, then the parties are called principal and independent contractor, and the financial and other obligations mentioned above do not apply. Another way of looking at the control question is to ask whether the work required is an *essential and integral part of the enterprise, or only an ancillary or incidental feature of it*. If the work is a vital part of the enterprise then it is governed by a contract of service, i.e., employment, but if not the contract is 'for services'. Since by definition the services are provided by someone who is not part of the main business enterprise, he is again classed as an independent contractor. For example, a window-cleaner is the employee of the firm which sends him to clean the factory windows, but so far as the factory occupier is concerned he is an independent contractor.

The test of control is a very general one whichever way it is used, and it needs explaining and qualifying in several ways. Firstly, the employer is not necessarily the person who actually gives the orders. Usually these are given by the supervisor, but he speaks on behalf of the employer. Again, it is quite possible that no orders have in fact been given regarding a particular operation. Lastly, the fact that the master may for practical purposes be unable to give orders, having less expert knowledge than the servant, does not affect the general rule. The test may therefore be more clearly stated as 'who has the *ultimate authority* to say what job shall be done, and how it shall be done?' That person or, as it is more often, that limited company is the employer. If no such orders can be given, the work is done on an independent or self-employed basis.

Whether a particular worker is an employee or an independent contractor can only be decided by reference to all the surrounding circumstances – *who pays, who gives orders, the nature of the orders, who can dismiss, etc.* All these are aspects of the degree of control exercised by one party over the other. Sometimes, as in the case of commercial representatives, the test may be very difficult to apply. The amount of discretion in the execution of orders may make a person an employee for some purposes and an independent contractor for others; Whittaker v. Minister of Pensions, 1966; A.E.U. v. Minister of Pensions, 1963 (union compelled member to act as 'sick steward' and exercised strict control over performance of these duties; member regarded as employee for national insurance purposes).

Two other important illustrations are the cases of Herbert v. Shaw, 1959, and In Re Hughes, 1966. Herbert, the plaintiff employee in the first case, was a skilled roofer. He had been working for one firm for several years, but he had originally offered his services as those of a self-employed man. For tax and national insurance purposes he was assessed as self-employed. Eventually he was injured at work, and claimed damages from the firm for which he worked on the ground that the firm had not complied with the Building Regulations.

The judge held that the references in the regulations to 'persons employed' clearly dealt only with the master and servant relationship. The plaintiff was therefore not protected by them, and lost his claim (A similar case is Inglefield v. Macey, 1967.) In the 1966 case, a number of workers sought to establish a claim for arrears of pay against a bankrupt building firm. The Companies Act, 1948, gives unpaid 'clerks, servants or workmen' a claim on the assets of a bankrupt employer before other unsecured debts are paid. These workers were members of a gang, recruited by a gang-leader. The leader accepted or rejected work from the firm on behalf of the gang, and distributed the work and payment. The firm made no P.A.Y.E. or insurance deductions for these men, nor did it control their hours of work. It was held that the Act only gave employees as such a preferential claim on the company's assets, and that these men were not employees of the company. Employers may seek to avoid selective employment tax, redundancy, and other insurance contributions by encouraging employees to classify themselves as self-employed, but these cases illustrate the many disadvantages for the worker in terms of safety and social security.

DIVISION OF LIABILITY

Normally, once we have established that a contract of employment exists, all the consequential rights and duties – notice, national insurance, safety liabilities, etc. – remain with the same employer. Exceptionally, however, one person might be the employer for national insurance or similar purposes, as in the A.E.U. case and in Morren v. Swinton Council, 1965 (local authority's superannuation liability to engineer under contract to consultants), while other responsibilities, e.g. for safety, may be imposed on some entirely different body.

HIRING-OUT; GENERAL AND PARTICULAR EMPLOYMENT

This division of responsibility may occur where labour is hired out from one employer to another. The usual or 'general' employer may continue to pay wages, stamp cards, and retain the right to dismiss, but the hired men may conform so closely to the temporary or 'particular' employer's conditions of work, and be so closely supervised by him, as to become for safety purposes his employees. This does not happen very often, but may arise if the hired labour is not highly skilled – thus requiring more supervision – and brings little or no capital equipment from the general employer, over which the general employer might be supposed to retain rights of disposal. (Mersey Docks and Harbour Board v. Coggins, 1946 – dock board crane and driver hired out to stevedores – stevedores not liable when driver caused injury; Denham v. Midland Employers' Assurance, 1956 – particular employer liable to unskilled hired man, but not entitled to be reimbursed by his own employers' liability insurance policy, which only covered liability to employees as such; Garrard v. Southey, 1952 – particular employer liable to electrician working on his premises). Such liability might also arise under one or two provisions of the Factories Act, e.g. section 29 (page 75).

If the general and particular employers determine in advance their liability in the event of an accident, this does not affect any injured person who is not a party to the agreement. He would sue whoever appeared to be liable under the general rules set out above, or both if in doubt, and the employers would then settle the matter between themselves in accordance with the terms of the contract of hire and the circumstances of the case.

APPRENTICES

We have now established how the law distinguishes employment from other working relationships. It only remains in this section to observe that apprentices are classified as employees for all relevant purposes – insurance, the Contracts of Employment Act, safety duties and the like – dealt with in subsequent pages. The special features of contracts of apprenticeship are that they must be in writing, signed by the apprentice, and be primarily for the purpose of teaching. A premium is not required by law. To be enforceable against an apprentice, the contract must not contain unduly burdensome terms, such as the employer's exclusion of safety liabilities. But if the contract is on the whole for the apprentice's benefit, it may properly contain disciplinary rules or other reasonable restrictions. An employer can only lawfully end a contract of apprenticeship if the apprentice breaks the express and basic terms of the contract, or otherwise makes teaching impossible. He has not got the same broad rights of dismissal with or without notice as he has over adult employees; Newell v. Gillingham Corporation, 1941.

The Form of the Contract

GENERAL RULE AS TO WRITTEN CONTRACTS

The general rule of English law is that a contract's validity does not depend on writing. A valid contract may equally well be made by word of mouth, or even by conduct. But if the contract is not written, practical difficulties may arise in proving what was agreed. For that reason it is always *preferable* to express contracts of any value or complexity in writing. This has been industrial practice for many years, i.e. by outlining the main conditions of employment such as overtime requirements and safety duties in works' rules booklets. These will be referred to in more detail under 'Terms', below.

The Contracts of Employment Act

Apart from this practical question of proof, however, there are a number of specific exceptions to the general rule that writing is not necessary. As mentioned earlier, contracts of apprenticeship must be in writing. Again, an employer can only legally fine, suspend or search his employees if he has previously claimed such powers in writing, usually in the works' rule book or by some prominently displayed notice. The rules as to fines of manual workers are set out in section 1 of the Truck Act, 1896, which requires that the grounds for such punishment must be adequately stated, that the fines must be fair and reasonable, and that the employee must receive written particulars of the deduction. The same rules apply to deductions for bad workmanship. Section 66 of the Mines and Quarries Act, 1954, is a statutory example of the need for writing before a search can be carried out. Another statute requiring writing for one part of the contract is the Payment of Wages Act, 1960, which obliges manual workers who want their wages paying by cheque to make written application to the employer. Regarding termination of the contract, *see* pp. 19 and 23.

The most substantial requirement as to writing, however, is in the **Contracts of Employment Act, 1963.** This Act, which was intended to foster security of employment, requires that certain basic terms of most contracts of employment shall now be stated in writing. It also changed the law regarding notice; this point is dealt with on p. 33. The Act declares (section 4) that **within thirteen weeks of beginning work, an employee shall be given a written statement which either contains or refers him to another document containing the following particulars: the date when employment began; rate and intervals of pay; hours; holidays and holiday pay; sickness and sick-pay; pension; notice (or, if employment is for a fixed term, the date the contract expires).** Essentially the Act provided that what might previously have been agreed orally should now be stated in writing. It did not, except with regard to notice, make or envisage any changes in the terms already agreed. The Act did not, for instance, mean that sick-pay schemes should be introduced where none previously existed, but only that the presence or absence of such schemes should now be clearly stated. On the other hand, the mere fact that these particulars have now to be in writing does not mean that problems of interpretation are ended. The written statement may still require the employee to work 'reasonable overtime', and the precise meaning of that and similar phrases must often remain in doubt.

COLLECTIVE AGREEMENTS

As stated above, the Act allows the employer to give a written statement which does no more than refer employees to some other more comprehensive statement which they have reasonable opportunity of inspecting, such as a copy of a collective agreement in the works office. If a collective agreement is referred to, its terms become part of the individual's contract of employment and he can then sue or be sued upon them, which he might not otherwise be able to do (N.C.B. v. Galley, 1958; Camden Exhibition v. Lynott, 1966; Silvester v. National Union of Printing Workers, 1966, and *see* p. 20). The Act leaves the employer free to impose or negotiate such changes as circumstances may require. The only requirement is that employees must receive a written statement of these changes within one month *after* they have been made. Or, if a single reference document is made use of, then it is sufficient to record the changes on that alone.

Questions as to the provision or correctness of the written particulars may be referred to an industrial tribunal; *see* p. 29. But the tribunal is only empowered to declare the parties' rights, not to enforce them. One side or the other must then take the case to the county court. The tribunal procedure is accordingly very little used. The employer's failure to give a written statement does not affect the existence of the contract, but only makes its terms more difficult to prove.

The Act applies to employees as defined under 'Parties', above, with these exceptions: part-time employees (i.e. those working under twenty-one hours a week); registered dock workers; seamen; Crown servants; employees who normally work abroad; employees who already have the specified details in writing; and employees who are closely related (father/mother/husband/wife/son/daughter) to the employer.

The Terms of the Contract

WORKS' RULES BOOKS

We turn now to the content of the agreement. The terms of the contract of employment – whether in an informal spoken agreement, or stated in the works' rules booklet, or in the written particulars required by the 1963 Act – are almost entirely a matter for voluntary negotiation between management and labour. The employer is not obliged by law to consult employees in drawing up their conditions of work, since the theory is that they are free to accept or reject his terms by staying on at or leaving that particular employment. If they remain at work, they are taken to have accepted the terms. The details of the contract may therefore often be seen as the product of passive acceptance. Signature or other receipt for works' rules books or the written statement is not a legal necessity, though the employer may require it if he wishes. If he does require it then at least he will be able to prove that he has issued the statement.

CHANGING THE TERMS

We have seen that the Contracts of Employment Act permits the employer to change the details of the written statement. He has the same rights regarding any other conditions of employment. In works' rules books, for example, management often expressly reserves the right to change the terms it has laid down. The exercise of this right is subject only to the pressures of good industrial relations. These two examples are equally lawful, once accepted by the employees: 'The Board reserves the right to alter or rescind any of these rules after consultation with the Works Council'; 'The Company reserves the right to make alterations to these rules at any time without notice'.

EXPRESS AND IMPLIED TERMS

Despite the long-standing practice of issuing works' rules booklets, and the more recent requirements of the Contracts of Employment Act, the fact remains that a great many problems are bound to arise at work which either cannot be expressly dealt with in advance, or perhaps their solution may seem so obvious as not to be worth stating. An example we shall return to shortly is the proposition that orders shall be obeyed. This would not usually be expressly stated in a contract, however essential it might be to the success of the enterprise. But the fact that the duty is not stated does not mean either that it does not exist, or that problems of disobedience may not arise. As well as the express terms, therefore, the law is sometimes prepared to add in other terms or duties to give effect to the basic purpose of the contract. These are called *implied terms*. They are none the less real obligations, whose breach could have the same consequences as breach of an express term, i.e. a claim for damages and/or summary dismissal. Some of the terms directly concern the supervisor, since it is his responsibility to see they are carried out. Because the express terms differ from contract to contract, it is only possible to consider in detail the implied terms, which are common to all contracts of employment *unless clearly excluded*. We shall look in turn at the implied duties of the employer and employee.

EMPLOYERS' IMPLIED OBLIGATIONS

Safety

Perhaps the most far-reaching of the implied obligations imposed on the employer are those concerning safety. These duties are imposed by both common law and statute, and are dealt with at length in Chapters 2 and 3. It is only necessary to observe here that substantial awards of damages may follow if the duties are broken.

Provision of Work

Generally the employer will not be liable for failing to provide work (Browning v. Crumlin Valley Collieries, 1926), unless he deliberately makes it impossible to continue work already contracted for, e.g. by selling out; Collier v. Sunday Referee, 1940. But as regards apprentices, employees paid partly or wholly by commission, and possibly pieceworkers, an employer might be in breach of contract if work were not available. The situation would normally be dealt with by an express agreement as to basic rates.

Payment

Another implied term is that the employer will pay for work done at the agreed rate until one side or the other ends the contract. The rate may be incorporated into the individual's contract by the express or implied observance of collective agreements, e.g. by the terms of the contract or the custom of the trade, or by an Industrial Court order made under the Terms and Conditions of Employment Act, 1959, a wages order made under the Wages Councils Act, 1959, or under a statutory rule such as the Dock Workers Order, 1967. The employee cannot claim as of right a payment which has always been stated to be within management's discretion, however often and regularly it may have been made; Grieve v. Imperial Tobacco, 1963. The employer must pay for work done in circumstances which normally give rise to payment. If no rate of pay is agreed, the servant can sue for the value of his work. The Contracts of Employment Act entitles a man to his pay when under statutory notice (p. 23) even though he may do no work for it – either because no work is available or because he is ill or on holiday (section 2 and schedule 2 of the Act). In passing, the employer is not obliged to give holidays with pay. This matter again is almost always expressly dealt with in the contract or, e.g. under a Wages Council order.

Indemnity

Where a man incurs expenses on his employer's behalf he is normally entitled to be indemnified. This right extends only to payments he has properly made in the course of employment, and not, for example, to costs incurred as a result of careless driving (Lister v. Romford Storage, 1956), or through exceeding instructions (Clitherow's Trustee v. Hemingway, 1966). The injured third party's rights against the employer are not affected by this rule; p. 51. The employer's duty to indemnify his employee does not give rise to an automatic right to compensation for injuries sustained in the course of work. Compensation here generally depends upon proof of negligence (Alveran v. Leonard, 1965).

Sick-pay

Again subject to any express or implied term to the contrary, a man who is off sick is entitled to be paid his normal wages until the contract is ended (Orman v. Saville Sportswear, 1960), though the rate clearly depends upon how far his pay derives from his presence at work. A waiter, for example, could not claim from his employer the value of tips lost through illness.

Restraint of Trade Terms

Many contracts of employment contain 'restraint of trade' terms. These are terms by which the firm or company expressly seeks to protect itself against the consequences of the employee's departure, e.g. by requiring him as a condition of employment not to take up similar service within so many miles or for so many months or years.

The position here is that whatever may be expressly agreed is subject to an implied term of *reasonableness*; otherwise it is invalid. Usually the task of proving the restraint was reasonable falls upon the employer, since almost always it is he who sues the former employee for an injunction or damages after the employee has broken his promise. Restraints are reasonable which provide 'no more than adequate' protection of the employer's proprietary rights, notably his trade secrets and business connections; Foster v. Suggett, 1918; Brunning v. Bentley, 1966. He cannot protect himself against the mere possibility of future competition from an ex-employee, nor from that man's exercise of his own skills, however much they may have been learned in that employer's service. If the restraint is too wide, the employer will normally be unable to enforce it (Gledhow v. Delaney, 1965) even though he may in fact have some genuine interest to protect (Commercial Plastics v. Vincent, 1964). In theory the judges also consider how far the public interest is affected by the restraint. Thus in Wyatt v. Kreglinger, 1933, an employee was held unable to enforce his claim to a non-contributory pension because it was conditional upon his abandoning his trade completely, and this was regarded as undesirable from the public point of view. But in Bull v. Pitney-Bowes, 1966, the judge simply struck out a similar restraint term from the pension scheme as being itself against the public interest, and the employee's claim was upheld.

Where rival employers agree between themselves not to employ each other's ex-employees, this is still a type of restraint of trade agreement, to which the same rule of reasonableness applies. As before, the law's emphasis is on the precise terms of the contract, e.g. whether it distinguishes between employees who may pass on trade secrets and those who cannot, rather than on any more general questions of public policy such as the restrictions on the employee's prospects or the elimination of competition (Kores v. Kolok, 1958). Agreements restricting the supply of goods, as distinct from services, are the concern of the Restrictive Practices Court.

References

It should be noted finally that an employer is under *no* duty to give references to or for ex-employees. His refusal may make it difficult to obtain another job, but there is no legal ground for complaint. On the other hand, the law does try to encourage employers to make such statements by relieving them of the consequences of defamatory remarks – so long as they are made in good faith; Hambrook v. Law Society, 1967. The employer has a duty to anyone likely to rely on his statements, such as a prospective employer, to ensure that the reference is not harmfully misleading; Hedley Byrne v. Heller, 1963.

EMPLOYEE'S IMPLIED OBLIGATIONS

We shall consider now the implied duties of the employee. As stated above, breach of these duties may entitle the employer to dismiss the servant without notice and/or to claim damages from him if he has suffered any loss. But the employer's rights must not be interpreted too strictly or literally. Their exercise is subject to common-sense rules as to the significance of the breach – as well as to labour reactions. These considerations are 'whether the acts and conduct of the party evince an intention no longer to be bound by the contract . . . In every case the question of repudiation must depend on the character of the contract, the number and weight of the wrongful acts or assertions, the intentions indicated by such acts and words, the deliberation or otherwise with which they are committed or uttered, and on the general circumstances of the case' (General Billposting Co. v. Atkinson, 1909).

Obedience

The implied obligation upon the employee to obey orders has already been mentioned as an example of the fundamental nature of implied terms, p. 9. The rule is that wilful disobedience of a lawful and reasonable order is a breach of contract. Apart from possible dismissal or a claim for damages, such a breach might also enable the employer to defeat a claim for damages for injuries caused partly through disobedience. In Harris v. Tyer, 1966, for instance, the widow's claim for damages for the death of her husband – a night watchman – through poisoning from gas-fire fumes was rejected because he had been asleep on duty. 'Wilful' signifies a deliberate flouting of authority, including abuse or other flagrant incivility, but probably not a single outburst of bad temper and still less some minor difference of opinion or disobedience based on inadvertence (Laws v. London Chronicle, 1959). A 'go-slow', as distinct from a 'work to rule', is technically disobedience. Orders which are not 'lawful and reasonable' may lawfully be disobeyed. If the employee does disobey such an order and is then summarily dismissed, he has a claim for damages for wrongful dismissal, p. 21. There seem to be two categories of 'unlawful' orders: those involving some risk of injury over and above that normally inherent in the work (*see* N.C.B. v. Hughes, p. 19), and those requiring the servant to do work which he was not employed to do. The latter question turns essentially on the definition of the particular job.

This extract from a shop steward's report in a trade union journal conveniently illustrates a problem of unjustified disobedience and accurately summarizes the legal position: 'Then we had a case where in defiance of an agreement providing for the interchangeability of labour in emergencies, a number of women members declined to fill the gaps caused by sickness in another department. True, the work was dirtier; but the transfer would only have been for a few hours. The manager dismissed the women, as he was entitled to do. Naturally we approached him for their reinstatement. He agreed to do so provided they took the jobs they had previously refused. "We must have a measure of flexibility," he said, "and I must maintain discipline. That would be impossible if these women were permitted to evade their turn to change jobs temporarily in times of need." So there was nothing for it but to inform the women that we could do no more.'

Competence

If an employee is unable to do the work he was taken on to do, he may be summarily dismissed. Whether the employer's dissatisfaction is genuine depends on the facts of each case. Considerations such as length of service, previous criticism, etc., are clearly important.

Another kind of disability may arise through illness. The question here again is whether the absence 'strikes at the root of the contract'. If the employee's job is one in which his personal skill or knowledge is all-important, then a very short period of absence or other slight reduction in his ability to do the work might justify summary dismissal (Condor v. Barron Knights, 1966 – illness of star drummer in pop group – dismissal without notice justified). But if the job can be filled by someone else without undue difficulty or loss, summary dismissal after even a lengthy absence might not be justified. In Storey v. Fulham Steelworks, 1907, a works manager who had been ill and absent for five months during five years' service agreement was dismissed without notice. His claim for damages for wrongful dismissal was upheld. Storey's case should, however, be contrasted with the Australian case of Simmons v. Hay, 1964, which probably represents the modern approach more accurately. Here an engineer was appointed under a three-year contract which obliged him to attend personally to his work. After ten months he fell ill. His salary was paid during the following seven months' absence, and then he was summarily dismissed. His claim for damages was rejected on the ground that his unfitness was permanent and 'would result in (his) being no longer able to perform the agreed services . . . for much the greater part of the agreed period of employment'. Leaving aside any possible right of summary dismissal, it should be borne in mind that an employer is not obliged to keep a post open indefinitely. *Almost every contract of employment provides for termination with the appropriate notice and if the employer chooses to give this because of his employee's absence through illness, no legal liability can fall on him, unless the contract expressly so provides.* As to sick-pay while the contract is still in force, *see* Orman v. Saville Sportswear, 1960, above.

Care

The employee must do his work carefully, and may be required to indemnify his employer against loss caused by his carelessness, even if the employer is insured against that loss; Lister v. Romford Storage, 1956. What degree of carelessness gives rise to liability is difficult to say, except in general terms that it is likely to involve injury or material financial loss to the employer; Baston v. London Printing Works, 1899. In Superlux v. Plaisted, 1958, it was held that an employee must take at least as much care of his employer's goods and interests as he would if they were his own – a very high standard. The judge decided here that the employee, a commercial representative, should have taken the goods with which his employer entrusted him into his own home, despite the inconvenience, instead of leaving them overnight in a van from which they were stolen. The employee was accordingly liable for the value of the goods, some £315. Similar cases concern thefts from vehicles left unlocked or unguarded. If the loss or damage to the employer were caused partly or wholly through the employer's own fault, e.g. in failing to provide necessary supervision, then his compensation would be reduced accordingly; Jones v. Manchester Corporation, 1952.

Good faith

The duty of faithful service broadly requires that employees shall work honestly and diligently, and that their financial interests shall not conflict with their employers. Works' rules often expressly prohibit 'industrial misconduct', either by cataloguing such acts as insubordination, gambling, interfering with machinery, private trading, lateness, slacking, overbooking, stealing, and the like, or by some more comprehensive condemnation such as: 'Any act of misconduct will render the offender liable to suspension or instant dismissal at the discretion of the Company'. But whichever way the problem is tackled difficulties of definition still arise. Each case has to be looked at on its own merits to see how far the conduct complained of is compatible with the completion of the work and the maintenance of authority.

Where a shop manager borrowed £15 from the till, leaving an I.O.U. for that amount in the till and replacing the exact sum the following day, his conduct was held to justify summary dismissal. He knew that his employer would not have permitted the 'loan'. As between master and servant, therefore, such conduct would be dishonest, even though not intended to be so. 'It was incumbent upon him as manager to keep the till inviolate. Those who have experience of the criminal courts know what happens once there is a departure from that principle' (Sinclair v. Neighbour, 1966). The employee must look after the customer's or client's interests on behalf of his employer, and not, for example, arrange to take that client's business privately; Sanders v. Parry, 1967. In a recent Canadian case, Protective Plastics v. Hawkins, 1965, the employee had within the four months before he left work arranged to join a competitor, collected confidential information for him from his employer, had told customers but not his employer that he was leaving, and generally had neglected his work. This conduct was held to entitle the employer to recover one-third of the salary paid within that period.

It is clearly a breach of contract to disclose confidential information about one's employer's business, whether for bribes or under union pressure (Bent's Brewery v. Hogan, 1945), unless possibly there is some question of public policy involved. Employees must account for all profits and confidential information received properly or improperly on their employer's behalf; Cranleigh Engineering v. Bryant, 1964; Reading v. Attorney-General, 1951. An employee might be subject to summary dismissal if he failed to disclose information about fellow-servants' dishonesty, particularly if he himself were in a responsible position; Swain v. West, 1936.

Interviews. How far does good faith require a person applying for a job to disclose facts about himself which might prejudice his application? If he is taken on as a commercial traveller, and the employer subsequently discovers he has a conviction for drunken driving, can he be summarily dismissed? The law's view is that the employer should ask about the matters he thinks are essential, and if he does not, then in the absence of fraud, the employee's failure to tell him is not a breach of contract; Hands v. Simpson, 1928; Bell v. Lever Bros. 1932. Keeping silent about one's fitness or otherwise for a job might, of course, contribute to an injury, in which case the worker would probably lose part of his damages; Cork v. Kirby McLean, 1952; Coles v. English Abrasive, 1965.

Spare-time activities. An employee's spare-time activities may possibly amount to a breach of faith with his employer. Some firms expressly forbid or reserve the right to forbid 'moonlighting' – spare-time work (e.g. 'the firm reserves the right to raise with an employee the question of outside work if such work is interfering with his efficiency'), and as mentioned earlier if the servant continues in employment then any such provision is binding upon him. But even without a term of this kind, the law may still intervene and stop spare-time activities if they seriously reduce a man's ability to do a good day's work, e.g. through fatigue, or if they involve competition against his employer. Clear evidence is required of direct competition in a specialized field of business, or of a division of loyalties on the servant's part, or of a substantial drain on his time or energies. Both manual and professional workers are affected by this rule, as shown by the cases of Hivac v. Park Royal Scientific Instruments, 1946 (breach of faith for skilled manual workers to work for rival in highly specialized industry on Sundays) and Bartlett v. Shoe and Leather Record, 1960 (breach of faith for editor to make numerous contributions to other journals on topics including those covered by own trade journal).

Other out-of-hours activities may also be relevant if they reflect directly or adversely upon one's work. Violent or dishonest behaviour, and convictions for such behaviour, would probably justify instant dismissal from almost any occupation; Tomlinson v. L.M.S. Railway, 1944. Conduct which is otherwise lawful may be inappropriate for particular livelihoods, e.g. immorality, drunkenness, or heavy gambling when employed in a position of trust; Pearce v. Foster, 1886.

Inventions. The test of faithful service may also determine who is to benefit from employees' inventions. If a man is employed to invent, the master is well advised to state expressly in the contract of employment what the parties' rights shall be. He is entitled to claim the whole benefit for himself, though many employers make appropriate payments under 'suggestion schemes'. But if the matter is not dealt with expressly, implied terms may resolve the problem. These require the employee to disclose inventions arising directly from his employment as an inventor ('Get out another design' – Adamson v. Kenworthy, 1932; Cranleigh Engineering v. Bryant, 1964), or as an incidental result of his researches (British Reinforced Concrete v. Lind, 1916), or where, though there are no express instructions, the employee works in a problem-solving capacity and is thus generally bound to find and disclose ways of furthering his employer's interests (Homewood v. British Syphon Co., 1956 – chief technician invented improved syphon through own interest – employer entitled to patent rights). If the employer has a claim to the patent rights under either express or implied terms of the contract, he can still make that claim against the servant even though the latter may have left work in order to patent the invention for himself. But the idea of the invention must have occurred during that service and it must arise directly out of the nature of the employment – both of which are questions which can only be decided on the facts of any particular case. The employer can apply for the patent rights even if the employee refuses to do so (Patents Act, 1949). Rights to benefit may be apportioned between the parties if it is impossible to say which is entitled to the whole benefit of the invention.

Ending the Contract

A contract may be ended in a variety of different ways, but the two most important are by carrying it out in accordance with its terms, or, equally effective in its own way, by breaking those terms. We shall look first at the consequence of breaking a contract of employment.

EMPLOYEE'S BREACH OF CONTRACT

If an employee has broken an important express or implied term of his contract, e.g. by disobedience or carelessness, he may be dismissed without notice. All money owing to the servant to the date of dismissal must be paid.

As a matter of law, the employer need not give his reasons for dismissal at the time he orders it, nor usually need he hear the employee's side of the case. He should nevertheless have some good reason for his action in case the employee sues for damages for wrongful dismissal. At the moment one of the results of summary dismissal is that the worker loses all existing entitlement to redundancy benefit, based on previous years of service. It is debatable whether an isolated act of misconduct should cause the loss of a possibly quite substantial right of this kind, and perhaps in these circumstances some discretion should be given to the redundancy tribunals. Apart from his right of summary dismissal, *an employer who has suffered material loss because of the worker's breach of contract may also sue for damages.* Such claims are comparatively rare today, but are by no means unheard of. The damages are calculated by reference to the direct and likely consequences of the employee's acts; N.C.B. v. Galley, 1958. In N.C.B. v. Hughes, 1959, a group of miners refused to work at a coal face which they claimed was exceptionally dangerous. The judge found that it was not so and therefore that their refusal was unjustified, i.e. a breach of contract. Each miner was accordingly held liable to pay £37, the value of his output during the shift he should have worked. Similarly, if a person is accepted for a job which starts at a later date and he fails to arrive on that day, that also is a breach of contract and he could be sued for management's expenses in finding a necessary replacement. But the fact that the law provides these remedies does not mean that either summary dismissal or claims for damages are necessarily wise courses of action to pursue, since both carry risks of strong labour reaction, allegations of victimization, and so on. Although summary dismissal may be justified, it may still be preferable to give a man notice, or money in lieu. If notice is given in these circumstances, the employer must now add a written statement that he has grounds for summary dismissal (Redundancy Payments Act, 1965). A further possible remedy against an employee who has broken his contract is an injunction. Thus a court order which may for example be used to stop an ex-employee from working for a rival in defiance of a valid restraint of trade term (*see* p. 11). It will not be used so as to compel a man to return to his former employment or to complete work in progress.

Strikes

It follows from what has just been said about claims for damages that if men walk out or strike without notice for any reason other than a breach of contract by the employer, they have each broken their contracts and in legal theory could each be sued for damages for the resulting loss to their employer. The same is true of strikes with notice since the notice is not intended to end the contract of employment but only to warn that the work will not be done; Morgan v. Fry, 1967. The so-called 'right to strike' is in fact an immunity conferred on those who organize the strike – usually, but not necessarily, the unions.

The terms of the immunity for those who cause others to break their contracts are laid down in the Trade Disputes Acts, 1906 and 1965. Section 3 of the 1906 Act declares: 'An act done in contemplation or furtherance of a trade dispute shall not be actionable on the ground only that it induces some other person to break a contract of employment.' This rule appears to exclude not only an employer's claim for damages against strike organizers, but also his use of an injunction to end a strike – Camden Exhibition v. Lynott, 1966. Immunity may again be given if there is some other legal justification, such as the protection of trade interests. If there is no such justification or if the Trade Disputes Acts do not apply because the broken contract is not strictly one of employment in the master and servant sense (Emerald Construction Co. v. Lowthian, 1966 – injunction granted against strikers seeking to prevent employment of *independent contractors*), both the organizers and the strikers themselves may be liable for deliberately or recklessly inducing breaches of contract between their employer and third parties.

Although these rights to sue for employees' breaches of contract are well-established, they are for practical reasons rarely exercised. Still less common has been the use of the criminal law, though until 1875 this was a standard method of dealing with 'unfaithful' employees. From then until recently the only relevant crimes have been 'wilful and malicious' breaches of contract likely to injure the public, e.g. by cutting off water, gas or electricity, or otherwise endangering life or property; Conspiracy and Protection of Property Act, 1875. But the possible criminal consequences of strikes are now greatly increased by the Prices and Incomes Acts, which make both unions and members liable to prosecution for striking or threatening to strike over prohibited wage claims.

EMPLOYERS' BREACH OF CONTRACT

Wrongful dismissal

The last aspect of breach of contract we shall consider is breach by the employer, such as non-payment of wages (Allen v. Thorn Electrical Industries, 1967), or wrongful dismissal. The worker's only remedy, apart from a right to leave without notice in the former case, is a claim for damages – unless against public policy or statutorily barred, as by the Prices and Incomes Acts, 1966 or 1967. So far as actions for wrongful dismissal are concerned, a successful employee has so far only been able to claim damages equivalent to his net earnings during the period of notice to which he was entitled.

The earnings claimed must be those the employee is bound to receive, which may include an allowance for tips or commission. But there is no claim for payments entirely within the employer's discretion, however likely such payment might be; Lavarack v. Woods, 1966. How far this sum might now be increased to represent loss of entitlement to notice under the Contracts of Employment Act (see p. 23) or to redundancy benefit (p. 28) is not yet established. On principle there seems no reason why these extra benefits should not be taken into account, and if they were they could substantially increase the sums usually awarded. It seems that the dismissed employee cannot claim compensation for other forms of loss such as damage to reputation (unless there is actual defamation) or difficulty in finding another job. His damages may even be reduced if the employer can prove that similar employment was reasonably obtainable elsewhere (Yetton v. Eastwoods Froy, 1966), and they will also be lessened by the amount of any unemployment benefit he may have received. The right to sue for damages for wrongful dismissal may therefore be an empty one in view of the time and expense and risk involved in making such a claim, particularly for the man who is only entitled to a week or two's notice. The necessary protection might be provided if the court or tribunal could order reinstatement for, say, six months, or compensation on that scale instead. As a rule English courts (unlike Continental ones) will not order reinstatement, but this is a possible remedy under the Dock Workers Order, 1967.

If without either party being at fault, circumstances change so that the contract becomes impossible to perform (not merely more difficult or expensive), the impossibility may – depending on the terms of the contract – have the effect of discharging both parties from their commitments, and such relief as seems just will be granted by the court.

FULFILLING THE CONTRACT

Notice

We shall assume now that the contract is in fact carried out by both parties. This may be done in many different ways, depending on the terms and purposes. A contract for a particular enterprise or for a specified length of time is fulfilled when the enterprise is completed or the requisite time has elapsed. But the most usual way of lawfully ending the contract is by one side or the other giving notice. The great majority of contracts expressly provide for termination by notice, and if they do not the law will normally imply a suitable provision. Thus *if notice or money in lieu is given in accordance with the terms of the contract it follows that such notice can never be a breach of the contract*; Austwick v. Midland Ry., 1909. Further, since the contract generally provides that either side may give, say, a month's notice, and since it does not usually specify when or why the notice may be given, *dismissal or resignation with notice may properly take place at any time and for any reason, or for no reason.* If on the other hand the grounds or procedure for dismissal are laid down, they must be strictly complied with. Exceptionally, a contract may be for a specified time, e.g. five years, and be silent as to the possibility of ending the contract before that time has elapsed. In that event, one party's termination of the contract within the five years might expose him to a very heavy claim for damages, representing the loss of earnings or loss of service, as the case may be, during the remaining months or years; Acklam v. Sentinel Insurance, 1959. Contracts of no fixed duration, e.g. from month to month, which do not provide for notice, are usually presumed terminable by a month's notice in the case of 'domestic servants', including club employees. For other employees the notice must be 'reasonable', which will depend on status, income, length of service, and the like, and may amount to several months for higher managerial posts. Contracts which make no reference to notice are very much the exception, particularly since the introduction of the Contracts of Employment Act in 1963, requiring written information on the point (p. 7). The contract itself may require notice to be given in writing. If it does not, written notice is only necessary for certain Redundancy Payments Act purposes (p. 26), and under the Dock Workers Order.

We have seen that the Contracts of Employment Act required written contracts so that employees should be certain more of the basic conditions of their work and so more secure. The second and perhaps more significant way in which the Act sought to improve industrial relations, to which we now turn, was by laying down *minimum periods of notice* – a novelty in English law.

Notice under Contracts of Employment Act. Before 1963, length of notice was a matter of mutual agreement, or, failing any express statement, the law would usually imply a 'reasonable' period, dependent on the factors mentioned above. For workers excluded from this part of the Act these considerations may still arise. Those excluded are employees normally working less than twenty-one hours a week; seamen; Crown employees; employees normally working abroad, and those whose contracts are for fixed periods of time. Dock workers were also excluded, but they now have similar protection under the Dock Workers Order, 1967. But most employees are within the Act, and their minimum rights to notice are laid down in section 1. The decisive factor is the length of service with the same employer, or anyone who takes over and continues his business. Section 1 provides that **after six months' continuous service, an employee is now entitled to at least one week's notice; after two years' – two weeks; and after five years' – four weeks.** Years of service before the Act came into force are included in the calculations. The notice appropriate to less than six months' service remains a matter for negotiation. The rate of pay during the statutory period of notice is decided by reference to the second schedule of the Act, which is also used for computing redundancy benefit and is referred to under that heading on p. 28. *See also* p. 11 as to entitlement to pay during absence through sickness, etc. To avoid penalizing long-service employees who may wish to improve their positions, *the Act only entitles the employer to one week's notice from an employee who has worked for him for any length of time over six months.* Either party may give money in lieu of notice, and either may voluntarily forego his right to notice. Contracts providing for more than the statutory periods are unaffected, but those which give less are amended so as to bring them up to these levels. *The Act does not in any way affect rights of dismissal or resignation without notice which arise on the other side's breach of contract; see* pp. 9–20

Continuous employment. We have seen that entitlement to notice under the Act depends on continuity of service. The Act states the effect on continuity of certain kinds of interruptions in employment. Absence due to holidays, sickness, injury, lay-offs or short-time does not affect continuity at all. Continuity is also preserved *even though the contract has been ended* in the following three cases: where an employee is dismissed because of illness and then re-engaged within twenty-six weeks of dismissal; temporary stoppages of work; absence from work in circumstances such that by arrangement or custom the employee is regarded as continuing in employment. These two latter cases may therefore enable an employee to get another short-term job elsewhere and then return to his original employer without losing his entitlement to notice. Both cases appear to depend on some mutual agreement to that effect. Time lost by other interruptions in service, notably strikes, is not counted. The original rule in the 1963 Act was that a strike without notice would end the contract altogether, but this was repealed by the Redundancy Payments Act, 1965. Finally, service of less than twenty-one hours a week, other than for illness, etc., as above, will sever the contract and all existing entitlement to notice is thereby lost. All these rules apply equally to the calculation of continuous service which has to be made under the Redundancy Payments Act; *see* p. 28.

The Contracts of Employment Act may be criticized on the ground that it does not go far enough to provide security in return for service. The periods of notice laid down could not be described as generous, and in particular they fail to make any provision for very long service. The man who has given twenty-five years of continuous service is not entitled by law to any more than the four weeks' notice he earned at the end of his first five years. But it should be remembered that these short periods are intended only as the absolute minimum to which a man is entitled, and contracts providing for longer notice are, of course, equally enforceable as well as being more beneficial to the cause of management–labour co-operation.

The general position at the moment, therefore, is that the employer's freedom to give notice is virtually unfettered by law. The only rule is that he must comply with the length of notice laid down in the contract, which as we have seen may be modified by the 1963 Act. This almost complete legal discretion is of course tempered in practice by the terms of collective agreements – e.g. that the union may require reasons to be given, or that a 'last in, first out' clause be operated – and more generally by the reactions of organized labour to dismissals. A probable future legal limitation is that dismissals because of union membership would be invalid. Great Britain is unusual in its lack of legal control over dismissals, which as a result often develop into industrial disputes. In many other countries the tendency has been to limit the employer's discretion and instead to regard a man's job as his property, loss of which may entitle him to compensation. In West Germany, for example, prior consultation with works councils is required by law. Other legal systems usually oblige the employer to offer some valid reason for giving notice, e.g. surplus labour, and if he cannot do this to the satisfaction of some independent tribunal or labour court, the dismissal is invalid. An interesting British development along these lines is provided by the Dock Workers Order, 1967, under which the employer must notify a local board of his intention to give notice, and the board may overrule him. Some countries provide a choice of compensation or reinstatement after unjustified dismissal, as in France, Belgium, Holland, and Norway. In the U.S.A. and elsewhere collective bargaining has reached much the same position, so that in effect dismissals can only take place for just cause.

THE REDUNDANCY PAYMENTS ACT

The only comprehensive exception to the two general rules of English law that the reasons for dismissal with notice will not be enquired into and that no legal consequences or claims can arise out of such dismissals is the **Redundancy Payments Act, 1965**. This is a very important Act, as much for the challenge it makes to previously undisputed employers' rights and the basis it may provide for eventual conformity with other countries' practices, as for what it actually does for the redundant employee.

The Act applies (with certain exceptions, p. 29) **to employees who are dismissed because the employer has ceased or is about to cease carrying on the business at that particular place or because the need for the particular work done by the employee within it has ended or diminished, or is about to do so** (section 1). An employer dismissed for one of these reasons, *and these reasons only*, now becomes entitled to compensation.

Dismissal

Two important points should, therefore, be noted. First, *there must be a dismissal*. Usually this means that the employer must give notice or dismiss without notice. But it may also cover the employer's refusal to renew a fixed-term contract, or his changing the conditions of employment so adversely to the employee as to give him grounds for leaving (Yetton v. Eastwoods Froy, 1966), or he may dismiss by offering the employee less suitable work with dismissal as the alternative. If the employee leaves of his own accord, even after a clear warning of likely future redundancy, he has no claim for redundancy payment since he has not been dismissed in any of these ways (Morton Sundour Fabrics v. Shaw, 1966). On the other hand a person is still regarded as dismissed if after receiving notice he gives in his own written notice in order to leave earlier – so long as this is not contested by the employer.

Redundancy following short-time work or lay-offs. The only exception to this requirement of dismissal concerns men who decide voluntarily to leave work because of short-time or lay-offs, other than that caused by industrial disputes (ss. 5–7). Short-time within the meaning of the Act occurs where less than half the normal week's pay is earned. It or the lay-off must have lasted for four consecutive weeks, or for any six weeks in thirteen. If the employee decides to leave because of these conditions he must within one month of the last of these weeks give his employer a written notice of his intention to claim redundancy benefit. 'Notice of intention to claim' (not required for dismissal as such) is different from notice to quit. Notice to quit must usually be given within the following four weeks, since redundancy payment is only made after the employment has ended. After the employer has been warned of the intention to claim payment, he may within seven days give a written counter-notice that he expects work to resume normally within four weeks. This serves as a warning that the employer will contest any subsequent claim for payment. Whether he will be able to do so successfully depends on the accuracy of his forecast of work.

Offer of alternative employment. There is no dismissal if within four weeks of giving his employee notice the employer offers to renew his contract or makes a written offer of suitable alternative employment (s. 2). His offer must be 'suitable in relation to the employee'. It should therefore take into account not only his previous rate of pay, status, training, and the like, but also any real domestic difficulties which might arise if the place of work is to be changed. If the alternative work is not suitable, or even if it is but there are circumstances such as ill-health in the family or difficulties over children's schooling which justify the employee in refusing the offer, then he is again regarded as dismissed because of redundancy.

Proof of Redundancy

The second vital point is that *dismissal must be because of redundancy*, as defined above. *By s. 9 all dismissals are presumed to be for this reason*, if there is no sufficient evidence to the contrary. If the employer wishes to avoid making redundancy payments it is for him, therefore, to show that they occurred for other reasons. Plainly if a man is dismissed for carelessness, disobedience, etc., he is not entitled to a redundancy payment. More difficult questions arise where after a reorganization of work an employee is unable to do the new or extra work and is then dismissed. In this case he may well be dismissed for incompetence, and not because the need for his work has ceased or reduced. The difference was discussed in North Riding Garages v. Butterwick, 1967, where the judge said that *redundancy only occurs if the overall requirements of the business have changed*. This does not necessarily mean that no new employees are taken on or that there are fewer jobs available. If the firm introduces new machinery, the new techniques required may lead to the replacement of older men by younger ones, perhaps even on a one-to-one basis.

Redundancy has still occurred here, even though the number of jobs has remained the same.

Benefits

The amount of the redundancy benefit is assessed, like entitlement to notice under the Contracts of Employment Act, on length of continuous service with one employer, or with an associated company, or with anyone who takes over and continues the business. As to the effect of interruptions in service, *see* p. 24. The minimum qualification is two years' work over the age of 18. Benefits are then payable in accordance with the first schedule of the Redundancy Payments Act and the second schedule of the 1963 Act. **For every year of continuous employment between the ages of 18 and 21, the redundant worker is entitled to half a week's pay. For every year between 22 and 40, one week's pay, and between 41 and 64 (59 for women), one and a half weeks' pay.** Each month's work in the last year before retirement reduces the redundancy payment by one-twelfth.

The week's pay, the basis of the redundancy payment, is defined as the 'minimum remuneration'. This refers to the rate of pay for the minimum number of working hours agreed in the contract. If the applicant claims that his week's pay should be assessed by reference to overtime rates, he must show that such overtime was a duty under the contract, and not merely that it was a frequent occurrence in practice; Pearson v. Jones, 1967. The timeworker's pay depends on his minimum earnings during his last working week, but the pieceworker's is based on his average earnings over the four weeks before notice was given. For shift workers and for those without normal hours, the average rate is based on the twelve preceding working weeks. In each case the above rule as to overtime applies.

Not more than twenty years' service is counted, including service before the Act came into force in December 1965. Weekly earnings will be disregarded by the extent to which they exceed £40. Thus the maximum possible benefit is £60 (£40 $\times$ 1$\frac{1}{2}$) $\times$ 20 = £1,200. The payment is made as a lump sum, free of tax, and does not affect entitlement to unemployment benefit. The employer must give a written statement with it showing how the amount has been calculated.

Disqualifications

The Act excludes various categories of employees from its scope. These are persons who contract to work less than twenty-one hours a week; employees whose notice expires on retirement at 65, or 60 for women; Crown employees (which does not refer to workers in nationalized industries); those employed under contracts of at least two years' duration made before the Act came into force; and employees who normally work abroad. An employee who is the husband or wife of the employer is also excluded, as are domestic servants who are close relatives of their employers. Apart from these categories benefit is as we have seen not payable to employees who before their notice expires unreasonably refuse the employer's written and detailed offer of suitable alternative employment. It may not be paid, or be paid only in part, in the following cases: where dismissal is for breach of contract, if the misconduct occurs while under notice for redundancy; where the employee goes on strike after dismissal and refuses a written request to make up the lost time; and where compensation is already due from other statutory or private redundancy or superannuation schemes. A claim will be lost if not made within six months after employment has ended.

Industrial Tribunals

All these questions, particularly whether dismissal was because of redundancy or for some other reason, and what constitutes suitable alternative employment, may be causes of dispute. The problems are to be resolved by industrial tribunals, composed of a legally qualified chairman, a representative of management, and a representative of labour. These informal tribunals were set up originally by the Industrial Training Act, 1964, to impose or rescind the training levies introduced by that Act. This great increase on their original work suggests that they could and (because of their cheapness and speed as compared with the ordinary courts) should be empowered to resolve any dispute over dismissal, with or without notice, thus helping to resolve these problems more amicably than now seems possible in this country.

Redundancy Fund and Rebates

Redundancy benefits are paid for directly by the employer. He must pay another 10*d.* per week on every male employee's insurance stamp and 5d. a week for every female. This money goes into a central Redundancy Fund. Despite this, however, the employer must still find the lump sum himself when he makes a man redundant, and he can then claim, depending on the man's age group, a rebate of either two-thirds or seven-ninths of the sum back from the Fund. If the employer will not pay the benefits, or cannot, e.g. through bankruptcy, the employee can apply to the Ministry of Labour for payment, and the Ministry then becomes a creditor of the employer.

How far is the Act likely to be successful in relieving hardship caused by the contraction of older industries and increasing automation? One administrative advantage is included in the Act, namely that employers must give details of anticipated redundancies to local employment exchanges at least two weeks before dismissals take place, or if more than ten employees at a time are affected, at least four weeks before. Some difficulties remain, however. One is that in effect employers may be penalized for modernizing, at least to the extent of one-third of their redundancy payments. Again, the employee in a declining industry is not encouraged to seek work elsewhere, but instead to wait as long as possible until he is actually dismissed (Morton Sundour v. Shaw, above). As the same case shows, employers who act in good (or bad) faith by warning their men of likely redundancies may only cause them to lose their redundancy payments. Further, the Act may not relate sufficiently closely to individual needs. Most awards will be for very much less than £1,200 and though welcome may still be inadequate to enable a man to face a long spell of unemployment. Or, on the other hand, a redundant worker may find another job within a very short time, in which case the benefit is largely unnecessary.

UNEMPLOYMENT INSURANCE

The answers to these problems seem to lie both in more generous retraining grants and in the concept of wage-related unemployment benefit which was introduced by the National Insurance Act, 1966. The criticism of the redundancy scheme applies in part to unemployment benefit, in that this also is payable only to those unemployed through no fault of their own, and generally not to those who leave voluntarily to improve their own prospects. But the new provisions at least relate much more to actual loss than the former flat rate of £4 a week, plus minor supplements for dependents, which was paid regardless of previous earnings or other commitments. This rate was approximately one-fifth of the national average wage. The 1966 Act increases national insurance contributions to provide supplements to the flat-rate unemployment and sickness benefits for a maximum of 156 days (six months excluding Sundays). The supplement is not more than £7 a week, i.e. one-third of earnings between £9 and £30 per week. Any earnings over £30 are disregarded. In no case will the flat rate and supplement exceed 85 per cent of a man's previous weekly earnings. The flat rate alone is payable for a further six months, after which the claimant must requalify for benefit by paying thirteen more contributions.

We have now examined what the law has to say about the contract of employment, in terms of standards of work laid down and expectations of honesty and fairness as between employer and employee. We shall consider in the next chapters perhaps the most complex problem arising out of the existence of the contract – the liability for injuries at work.

2: The Employer's Common Law Liabilities for Safety

At the beginning of the first chapter the distinction was made between the law made by Parliament – statute law – and that made by the judges – the common law. As regards safety at work, these two types of law may very well overlap, and yet are quite separate and distinct sets of obligations.

The obligations of the common law are much wider than those imposed by, for example, the Factories Act or Mines and Quarries Act. The common law covers all types and places of work, not just those processes or places selected as especially dangerous by Parliament. Indeed, only a minority of each year's thousands of industrial casualties are caused solely by breaches of this or that section of a statute, and most claims for damages turn partly or wholly on common law rights. We shall therefore deal first with this more comprehensive aspect of employers' liabilities. This in turn divides between the employer's personal duty *to* his employees, and (p. 51) his responsibility *for* them in their dealings with each other and with the outside world. For his duties to others on his premises who are not his employees, see the Occupiers' Liability Act, 1957; p. 96.

The Employer's Duty to his Employees

REASONABLE CARE

The duty the judges have devised and imposed on employers is a version of that which in broad terms we all owe to each other, to try to guard against causing injury (Donoghue v. Stevenson, 1932). The short and fundamental rule is that **'the employer must take reasonable care not to subject his employees to unnecessary risk.'** If he fails, the resulting claim for damages by the injured employee is based on the 'tort' or civil wrong of negligence, or possibly on the employer's breach of the contract of employment. Very occasionally, the employer may also be prosecuted by the State, if the negligence is particularly blameworthy and grave in its consequences.

The crucial question in all the cases we are about to consider is, of course, the meaning of 'reasonable care'. But before examining these cases, which explain in detail how the standard is applied, it may be helpful to consider these introductory points.

Test of Reasonableness

First, the requirements of safety on the one hand and production on the other must sometimes conflict. By the test of reasonableness the judges are able to bring more or less current and widely accepted ideas of fairness to assess the merits of both sides, and they seek with a high degree of impartiality to reach a working compromise between these conflicting interests. Secondly, the need for this compromise indicates that *the standard of reasonableness cannot amount to a guarantee of absolute safety*. It is quite possible to be injured through no fault of one's own, and yet to have no claim against the person who could be said to have caused the injury. A non-industrial illustration may clarify the point. If someone passing *your* house were injured because in a high wind a slate blew off your roof, when you had no reason to suspect that any of the slates were loose, would you expect to have to compensate him? The probable answer is 'no' – and that would be the law's answer also.

In Vickers v. British Transport Docks Board, 1964, the judge put the general position on employers' liability this way: 'The common law has always, rightly, been solicitous for the safety of workmen; but it has never pushed its solicitude to the point of saying that a employer is negligent merely because he asks his servants to perform work which is to some extent dangerous. If that were the law, many commercial activities would be impossible, the industrial life of this country would be stifled, and the very people whom the law is seeking to protect would probably be reduced to starvation.' (Whether these various arguments are at all convincing from the point of view of the injured person is perhaps more debatable. *See* p. 116 as to the question of absolute liability.)

Assessment of Liability

It follows that what is reasonable in any particular case can only be determined by such distinct but interrelated considerations as:

Inherent risk. As pointed out in the case above, all work carries with it some irreducible or irremovable element of risk, for which an employer cannot be held responsible. Driving even the newest and safest lorry remains a hazardous occupation, but most of the hazards of the road are beyond the employer's power to control, and accordingly he would not be liable to the driver for them. The limits on the employer's duty in such self-evidently dangerous jobs as steel-erecting and the like are still more clear.

Reasonably foreseeable risk. If the danger *could* be reduced or eliminated, the question remains whether the employer was negligent in failing so to do. As the earlier example of the falling slate shows, the law will not make a person liable solely because he could theoretically have prevented the accident. As a general rule, liability is only imposed when the accident was *likely*, or, in the usual phrase, 'reasonably foreseeable'; Bolton v. Stone, 1951. This means that the employer's actual or imputed knowledge of the risk is all-important. His knowledge and in turn his ability to prevent an accident may depend upon the supervisor communicating or otherwise acting upon complaints or other information from the shop floor.

It should be noted, however, that not all likely accidents or losses entitle the victim to compensation. He must also prove that his injury was the *direct* consequence of the employer's act or failure to act. If these two requirements do not coincide, as they usually do, the injured man has no claim. Some kinds of loss may be quite likely, for example, but the law does not see them as so directly related to the original act as to justify awards of damages. If the employer's negligence injures a worker, his fellow-employees are likely to lose work or pay, but they have no claim against the company for that loss. Similarly, there may be no doubt about the direct cause and effect of an accident, yet the law may again deny liability. In Doughty v. Turner Manufacturing, 1964, a workman negligently dropped an asbestos cover into a pit of molten metal. This caused an explosion which injured another employee. The judge held that since the explosion was not a reasonably foreseeable consequence of the original negligent act, the employer was not liable. For other examples of the problem, *see* 'Remoteness of Damage', p. 102.

Another important aspect of the judges' approach to negligence is that they are reluctant to be 'wise after the event', that is, to blame an employer for doing what at the time seemed right and necessary though it can later be seen as a mistaken decision. Saul v. St. Andrews Steam Fishing Co., 1965, which concerned a fisherman who was injured when working on the foredeck in a rough sea, draws a clear distinction between negligence and a mere error of judgment such as was said to have occurred here when the skipper ordered the work to be done despite the weather.

Obviousness of risk. The more obvious the danger, the more likely the law is to impose liability on the employer for failing to prevent the accident. But the hazard may be equally apparent to the employee, who can then be expected to take more care for himself – or else lose part or all of his claim under the rules of contributory negligence (*see* p. 104). Employers are not bound to stop employees from doing work for which they may not be suited, if the perils are obvious to the employees themselves (Withers v. Perry Chain, 1961; Jones v. Lionite, 1961 – no liability for death of employee through addiction to trichlorethylene vapour).

Seriousness of risk. 'The greater the risk, the greater the liability' is generally a valid statement of the law, but it may need qualifying. For example, it does not follow that liability will automatically be imposed if something goes wrong in a very dangerous process, such as in an explosives factory; Read v. Lyons, 1946. Proof of negligence is still essential. Again, if an unlikely accident would be bound to have very severe consequences if it occurred, the gravity of the consequences might be taken to outweigh the improbability of the event and so make precautions necessary. So in Paris v. Stepney Borough Council, 1951, the court held that goggles should have been provided for a one-eyed man although the danger was so slight that they would not have been required for a normally sighted person. The liability here also depended on the employer knowing of the disability and therefore of the need to provide special protection. In passing, we may note that at common law it is for the employee to disclose his disabilities, and not for management to seek them out.

Cost. It is important not only to discover the risk, but also to consider the method and cost of preventing or reducing it. The law would think it unreasonable to make an employer spend a fortune avoiding some slight possibility of accident. The cost of preventing even very serious and quite predictable injuries might still be too great in terms of the needs of society as a whole to make such precautions necessary. Where a man was electrocuted in the course of minor maintenance work on an electric railway, the court declined to say that the only possible precaution – turning the current off – should have been taken; Hawes v. Railway Executive, 1952. Any other conclusion would wreck the railway services, and every other enterprise with comparable risks. *Reasonable care depends essentially on what is practicable in all the circumstances.*

Employer's personal responsibility

The duty of weighing up all these factors and deciding what on balance is a reasonable course of action is cast by the law upon the employer. He, like the law, must decide each situation on its own merits. In legal theory this is a personal responsibility, and one which cannot be delegated. In fact, of course, in all but the smallest concerns there is substantial delegation of managerial authority, and so far as safety is concerned it is part of the supervisor's job to take the everyday decisions. The rules we are examining should serve as a guide to him in one of his most difficult tasks.

We turn now to consider some of the leading common law cases on employers' liability, drawn from many different kinds of employment. The cases are all applications of the one rule that reasonable care must be taken, but they are divided for convenience under the headings of premises, equipment, fellow-employees, and system of work.

SAFE PREMISES

The employer's duty to take reasonable care to provide a safe place of work is well illustrated by the case of Latimer v. A.E.C. 1953. The A.E.C. factory was flooded in an exceptionally heavy rainstorm, and after the storm a slippery deposit of water and machine oil was left on the factory floor. The circumstances were such that the employers had only two courses of action open to them in trying to make the place safe; either to close the factory completely, or to keep it running and protect the essential staff as best they could. They decided on the latter course, and put down all available sawdust. Unfortunately, there was not quite enough sawdust to protect all the employees who had to be at work if the factory were to be kept open. The plaintiff was one of the very few whose places of work were unprotected. He slipped and broke his leg, and then sued for damages for negligence. He lost his claim because it would be unreasonable to make employers close factories in order to ensure that their workers did not slip. His broken leg was, in the judge's view, simply a highly improbable consequence of an otherwise reasonable course of action. If, of course, the consequences of a possible slip could be plainly seen to be death or serious injury, this would clearly have outweighed the expense and inconvenience of closing the factory.

Complaints

Such an issue arose in Bath v. British Transport Commission, 1954. Here a man was working high up on a narrow dock-side ledge. He was not protected by any rail, belt, or net, nor was it the general practice in the industry to provide such precautions. He fell and was killed. It was held that his widow was entitled to damages. The danger was extreme and made no less so by the fact that other employers chose to ignore it, nor by the fact that neither the deceased nor his union had complained about it. (A complaint does not prove that work is dangerous any more than failure to complain proves it safe. On the other hand the presence or absence of complaints clearly provides useful evidence one way or the other.) Once this very real hazard was proved, it was for the employer to show that safety precautions could not reasonably be provided, and this he had failed to do. The measures might be drastic and expensive, but they were practicable.

Maintenance

These two cases usefully indicate both the range of risks and the law's response. There is no duty to take very substantial precautions to avoid a trivial risk, but where the risk is great every effort must be made to reduce it. Let us now apply these various considerations to more typical problems. If a man slips and injures himself on a pool of oil or water between the white lines on the factory floor, is the employer liable? We cannot answer 'yes' or 'no' immediately. Although he is walking where he is intended to, to say that that alone makes the employer liable would mean that he must catch every drop of oil before it hits the floor, or wipe every man's shoes as he comes in from the rain. We can only discover whether reasonable care was taken by finding out how the oil or water came to be there (for the best-kept machinery may still occasionally leak), how long it has been there, and whether the employer knew or should have known about it, and appreciated it as a danger (Richards v. White, 1957; Stowell v. Railway Executive, 1949). If the gangway is *frequently* slippery or there is some new and hidden obstruction then we can say with some certainty that management will be liable (Westwood v. N.C.B., 1967; Lewis v. High Duty Alloys, 1957; Light v. Bourne and Hollingsworth, 1963 – employer liable for not telling visiting contractor to keep narrow passage clear). Often enough the problem is simply one of 'good housekeeping' or an adequate maintenance system (Graham v. Distington Engineering, 1961 – failure to prevent sand on foundry floor from hardening into ridges – employer liable; Braham v. Lyons, 1962 – slippery substance on floor – maintenance man immediately on way to clean it up – another employee slips on it before he gets there – employer not liable; Vinnyey v. Star Paper Mills, 1965 – employee sent to clean up floor slips on it himself – employer not liable). In cases where the employer is primarily to blame, the employee may still lose some part of his damages because he must know that factory floors may have obstacles upon them, and should be on his guard against them. The employee will be still more clearly guilty of contributory negligence, probably to the point of losing his case altogether, if he is injured while doing something he is not supposed to do, e.g. taking a short cut between machines. The same general considerations apply to the employer's provision of a safe means of access to the workplace – the factory roadways, steps, passages, etc. – and to the safety of other ancillary areas such as canteens and toilets; Davidson v. Handley Page, 1945. *See also* ss. 28 and 29 of the Factories Act, p. 73.

Working away

The master's responsibilities to his servants continue when they are sent to work on someone else's premises. But since the premises are not his, the appropriate precautions may be different. They may be in the form of safety equipment (as in Christmas v. General Cleaning Contractors, 1952 – for window-cleaning employees), or instructions, either to one's own employees (Baker v. White, 1962 – another window-cleaning case), or to the occupier of the premises. In Bayliss v. Bournemouth Corporation, 1963, refuse collectors employed by the Corporation had complained to their foreman of the danger in carrying skips down a steep spiral fire-escape on a block of flats. Nothing was done, and eventually a man slipped and was killed. The supervisor's knowledge (unlike the shop steward's) is attributed by law to the employer, so that here the employer knew or ought to have known of a serious danger, but failed to take any action to prevent it. The Corporation was held liable because it could and should have required the occupiers of the flats to carry their own refuse down, or have the stairway altered. A similar case is Smith v. Austin Lifts, 1959, where liability was divided – 20 per cent on the employer who had failed to check whether a danger on the occupier's premises had been remedied, and 80 per cent on the occupier who knew of the danger but had not remedied it. Some Australian cases go further and suggest a general rule that the employer should through some appropriate representative *inspect* the premises where his men are sent to work; Sinclair v. Arnott, 1964. Lastly we may mention Cilia v. James, 1954, a case concerning a plumber electrocuted in an attic, which shows once again that an employer cannot be liable for totally unexpected dangers, whether on his own premises or someone else's. *See also* p. 96 as to the possible liability of the occupier in cases of this kind.

SAFE EQUIPMENT

Equipment, plant, and appliances cover all the things which a person may be expected to work on or with, ranging from machinery and safety equipment to, as in one case, a horse. The principles are the same as those just examined, and indeed many of the cases could fall under either heading.

A few brief examples of the many problems which are not covered by statute law will show the importance of the common law in remedying dangerous processes. In Bradford v. Robinson Rentals, 1966, the employer was liable for frostbite injuries caused to the employee after being ordered to drive 500 miles in freezing weather in an old van without a heater and with a leaking radiator. Smooth tyres and a defective fuel governor on a tractor have been grounds for liability in recent Australian cases. In Pellicci v. Jeyes, 1964, a packer contracted dermatitis when a new method of packing lavatory cleanser containing acid was introduced which involved for the first time contact between the operatives' hands and the cleanser. The defendant employers said they had not provided gloves at that time because there was no history of dermatitis being caused in the packing. But they were found liable because they should have known of the dangerous nature of their own product and should have anticipated that the new process might cause injury. In passing, other dermatitis cases such as Watson v. Ready Mixed Concrete, 1961, show that merely to issue barrier cream is not necessarily a sufficient answer to this very common industrial disease, since its effectiveness is known to vary widely with different processes.

General Trade Practice

The precautions taken by the rest of the trade are clearly a very relevant guide as to whether reasonable care has been taken in any particular case. There is a very heavy burden of proof upon the employee who tries to show that the general practice is at fault, but this can be done as we saw in Bath v. B.T.C., p. 37. 'One has always to have in mind that an established practice might be an established bad practice' (Sheridan v. Durkin, 1967). So in Welsford v. Lawford Asphalt, 1956, there was evidence of a general practice not to provide goggles for certain building work – chipping a brick wall – but the danger was held to be so obvious that the employer was none the less liable. Birnie v. Ford, 1960, is an unusual case in which the employers had taken precautions as good as or better than those of their competitors to protect press-shop workers, but were still liable despite the fact that they did not devise proper protection until some time after Birnie's injury. The danger of cuts from the very sharp panels of steel was an obvious one, and the time taken by the safety officer to provide suitable protection was evidence that the employers had been negligent.

Hidden Defects

If the defect in the equipment is not apparent on reasonable inspection, the *manufacturers* may be liable for it if caused through their negligence. Davie v. New Merton Mills, 1959, shows that where the equipment is an elementary and normally safe item (here, a drift) employers might discharge their duty of care simply by ordering it from reputable manufacturers, because they themselves could not reasonably be expected to do anything in the way of testing it. But employers should probably conduct their own tests before putting more complicated or dangerous equipment into service. Some doubt remains, however, as to the basis of the employer's liability for injuries caused by goods or services provided by an independent contractor.

Davie's case turned on the nature of reasonable care, but other cases depend on the point made on p. 36 that the duty to take reasonable care is one which only the employer can discharge, and not someone else on his behalf. This different approach to the same kind of problem leads to conclusions which do not appear to be reconcilable. Thus in Sumner v. Henderson, 1963 (reversed on appeal on different grounds, 1964), a shopkeeper was held liable for the death of his employee in a fire caused either by the negligent manufacture or negligent installation of electric wiring on his premises. Paine v. Colne Valley Supply Co., 1938, similarly made an employer liable for the negligence of an independent contractor.

Research and Testing

One last problem, implicit in many of the cases above, is that of the standard of knowledge, research, testing, and inspection which is expected of the employer. He is, broadly speaking, expected to keep up with trade and official reports, particularly those of the Factories Inspectorate; Balfour v. Boardman, 1956; Clifford v. Challen, 1951; Dickson v. Flack, 1953. But two isolated references in Factories Reports in 1935 and 1936 were held not to impute knowledge of the dangers of wood which was not imported in quantity until about 1950; Ebbs v. Whitson, 1953. If there is no suggestion that a process is or might be dangerous, then still more clearly the employer will not be liable if injuries occur, because he could not have known what precautions to take. So in Harman v. Mitcham, 1955, no blame was attached for a rare case of chronic poisoning, caused by the use of beryllium oxide in the manufacture of fluorescent lighting tubes. So far as the inspection and renewal of machinery are concerned, the employer must remember that what was once accepted as safe may no longer be so simply through the passage of time. The general tendency is always towards higher standards of safety; Lovelidge v. Odling, 1967; Barkway v. South Wales Transport, 1950 – an example of the very high degree of care imposed on a bus company to test its vehicles. The duty to inspect is summarized in a 1964 New Zealand case which concerned the collapse of a metal stand used instead of a hoist under a lorry: 'Employers clearly have an obligation to keep equipment in good order. Wear and tear affects all equipment, good or bad, and failing to inspect for this purpose the employer was unaware of the patent defect awaiting discovery, and thus omitted to withdraw the stand from use.'

SAFE FELLOW-EMPLOYEES AND COMPETENT SUPERVISION

This heading requires little more than the proposition that the employer must select suitably qualified people to do his work, provide training where it is necessary, and in particular see that those in charge have the knowledge and ability to see that the work is done safely. This responsibility is especially clear where young persons are employed. As the 1965 Report of the Chief Inspector of Factories put it, with all too many supporting cases: 'Many managements are still not careful enough in seeing that those appointed to supervise realize they should look after the safety of young people at all times. A few minutes' lack of supervision often brings disastrous results because of the failure of young persons to appreciate the hazards involved in seemingly harmless high-spirited pranks in and around their places of employment. Unfortunately, managements and supervisory staffs are inadequately prepared for their responsibilities—or, in some instances, simply ignore safe practices.'

Training

The duties to train and to ensure competent supervision are quite independent of any imposed by the Industrial Training Act, 1964, or any other educational programme. They apply at all levels and may be expressed in a great variety of different ways, as these quotations from judgments show: 'The employer must remember that men doing routine tasks are often heedless of their own safety, and may become careless about taking precautions. He must, therefore, by his foreman keep them up to the mark and not tolerate any slackness'; 'For a fitter... to make no effort to instruct his mate not to embark on a hazardous enterprise of this kind does amount to a serious lack of proper supervision'; 'If employers... put a young girl in charge of such a machine, they are under a duty of giving special instructions to her'. The duty to appoint people with particular qualifications for particular duties may be implied by the common law, as in Birnie v. Ford, above, and it may also be expressly laid down by Act of Parliament, e.g. where the Factories Act requires 'competent persons' to carry out various tests and inspections (*see* p. 78 on safety supervision), and in the Mines Act, 1954, which requires trained mine managers to be appointed.

Dangerous Employees

If the employer knows or ought to know, perhaps because of complaints, that certain employees are positively dangerous to others, then he is obliged to 'remove that source of danger' – just as he is obliged to attend to machinery and other such risks. Thus management has been held liable for the conduct of known bullies and practical jokers (Ryan v. Cambrian Dairies, 1957; Hudson v. Ridge, 1957), and persecution of one employee by another might possibly be actionable (Veness v. Dyson, 1965). But the element of foreknowledge of risk is, as in most common law cases, essential. So in Smith v. Crossley Bros., 1951, where apprentices seriously injured one of their number by injecting compressed air into him, there was no liability for failure to supervise them because this type of behaviour was said to be completely unforeseeable (though by the same token, it is now predictable). In contrast is Heffer v. Rover Car Co., 1964, where the judge held the employer partly to blame for fire injuries, saying: 'It might be that this particular form of larking would not have occurred to anyone looking into the possibilities of danger. But there was an obvious risk of larking taking place and an obvious hazard in allowing petrol to lie about in open cans.'

To a large extent this aspect of employers' liability has been superseded by the Law Reform (Personal Injuries) Act, 1948, p. 52. This Act makes the employer liable for the negligent acts of his employees *whether or not* he has failed in the personal responsibilities we have just considered. But the common law duty may still be relevant, because while the 1948 Act makes it a condition of liability that the acts complained of are committed in the course of employment (*see* p. 52), thus excluding bullying and skylarking, the different rules of the common law may still regard such acts as the fault of the employer.

SAFE SYSTEM OF WORK

This heading is perhaps the most comprehensive of all. It relates to the way in which the work is done – the 'setting of the stage' – the need for and nature of *instructions, adequate facilities for the job, safety training and equipment, and the like*. The problems may arise for a single operation just as much as for routine work. At the same time, the word 'system' does not always signify some very elaborate arrangement, but only that which is appropriate to the need. The basic problems are, first, when such regulation by the employer is necessary, and second, where the responsibility lies if instructions should be given but are not, or are given but ignored.

The law's conclusions correspond very closely with the facts of industrial practice. A supervisor would not expect to have to give minutely detailed instructions from moment to moment to an experienced man doing a routine job, even one involving some clear element of danger, nor, generally speaking, would the law require him to do so. As was said in Ferner v. Kemp Bros., 1960: 'An experienced workman must know the ordinary risks of the work which he is employed to do. In doing that work he is expected to take the ordinary routine precautions which are common to it, and should not expect to be told by his employer of every danger which might arise and every step that should be taken to counteract that danger.' Such persistence would clearly not only be impracticable, but also 'it would be regarded by a skilled man as an insult [for example] to give every fitter precise instructions how to carry out every routine job of maintenance because if he departed from the accepted method of doing the job his departure might involve an element of danger' (Ashley v. Esso, 1956).

These extracts from judgments help to show that *the employer's duty is to initiate and maintain a safe system where there is (i) a real risk of injury; (ii) some degree of complexity or unfamiliarity in the work; (iii) some practicable precaution*. To put these points another way, the employer will *not* be liable if he leaves the employee to use his own skill and discretion in tackling a straightforward and familiar job, and he then injures himself through doing the job foolishly or carelessly.

So, for example, an employer is not obliged to tell employees in a scrapyard not to hit an unexploded shell with a hammer (O'Reilly v.

National Rail, 1966), or not to put their weight on obviously rotten wood (Wilson v. Tyneside Cleaning, 1958), or to turn away from dangerous work when removing goggles (Foden v. Midland Motor Cylinder, 1966), or how to get on a works bus (Ramsey v. Wimpey, 1951), or how to avoid a rush into the canteen (Lazarus v. Firestone Tyre, 1965).

When a skilled steel-erector was instructed to erect a block and tackle on a roof truss 14 feet above ground, and fell because he was not using a ladder, no liability was imposed for the employer's failure to tell him to use a ladder, or to point out that a ladder would be safer; Brennan v. Techno, 1962. Nor was any blame attached when a worker who was told to cut a pipe with a hacksaw used a hammer instead and thereby injured himself, for this would have meant that the employer must anticipate disobedience of the clearest and simplest instructions; Langan v. French, 1961. In Winter v. Cardiff R.D.C., 1950, an employee was injured allegedly through the employer's failure to order that a heavy load be tied on a lorry. The employer was not liable because 'the matter was not either intricate or bewildering. It was not an enterprise calling for elaborate planning or precise and detailed instructions. The job required the exercise of judgment on the spot. It might almost as well be suggested that the tying up of every parcel in a shop is a matter for the employer's discretion.'

Lifting and Similar Injuries

Many injuries are caused through lifting or carrying loads beyond the employee's capacity. Apart from any statutory limitations (*see* p. 84), or other special considerations such as a known disability, the judges seem to accept that an adult male can be expected to lift a weight of at least 100 lb without thereby proving negligence against his employer. In a recent Australian case two men were instructed to lift a load of 160 lb from knee height to waist height. One was injured in so doing but the judge rejected his claim: 'To assert that a labourer may recover damages in tort because he is required to perform labour of a moderate kind . . . is completely unsupportable.' But if the job was patently too difficult, the tendency might be to say that the employee was foolish to go on with it. On the other hand, attention is paid to such factors as instructions or the lack of them, pressure of work, availability of help, and so on. In Ashcroft v.

Harden, 1959, the practice was to ask for help in lifting loads up to 150 lb which had to be done about once a day. It was sometimes necessary to wait for up to half an hour for labourers who were available for this purpose. The plaintiff waited for nearly half an hour for assistance in lifting a 150-lb load, and then tried to lift it himself although he knew it was beyond his capacity. He sustained a rupture. Held: no failure to provide a safe system. But the employers were liable when a man was left to deal with a load of 420 lb without being told how to use a crowbar, or that there were crowbars available, or that he should obtain help; Ioannou v. Fishers Foils, 1957; Hardaker v. Huby, 1962.

Two other cases illustrating the employee's duty to assess his own capabilities for the job are Adamson v. Ayr Engineering, 1963, where a fitter who was grinding the interior of a marine-engine cylinder was overcome by the heat, fainted, and injured himself, and Hall v. Peter McLaren, 1958, where a stoker contracted a hernia. In both cases the employer escaped liability. The reasoning in Hall's case applies broadly to Adamson's: 'It is a possibility that anyone whose work involves lifting heavy weights or the like may unfortunately contract that complaint. But when employers engage a stoker and set him to fire boilers, they must, I think, assume that he is the best judge of his own capabilities. If he makes any real complaint of the conditions on the score that they make the work dangerous, or are liable to cause injury to him in the way of strain, then it may very well be that if employers ignore such a complaint, they will do so at their peril.' Similarly, those who use the simpler types of equipment should be the first to recognize faults and it may be their responsibility to report them rather than the employer's to conduct periodic inspections (Bastable v. Eastern Electricity Board, 1956 – employer not liable for blunt chisel).

Inadequate Instruction or Equipment

There are, of course, a great number of cases which go the other way and make the master either partly or completely liable. Here the reasons for the liability are, e.g. that complex and dangerous machinery has not been regularly or properly inspected (Wall v. Barker, 1957 – failure to inspect mechanism of tipping lorry – employer liable), or that the employee has been left to face some unusual hazard without instructions, or to find for himself plant which might be unsafe and which is necessary for a difficult job. In Ross v. Associated Portland Cement, 1964, a chargehand steel-erector was told to repair an aerial ropeway, work of a kind he had not done before, and for which he was supplied only with a ladder. After the accident it was held that the employer was two-thirds to blame for providing inadequate supervision and equipment. The judge expressly took account of the very real factor of the man's 'natural reluctance to go uninvited to ask for extra equipment', but he still lost the remaining one-third of his compensation because, said the court, he ought not to have used the makeshift equipment. Littley v. Fairey Engineering, 1965, is another case on inadequate equipment, in which the proper standard of care is clearly stated. Here a capstan setter operator was injured by a ribbon of high-tensile steel which he was cutting. The employer had not provided any means of breaking up the steel ribbon 'so that serpentine coils 20 feet long, with their recognized and admitted potentiality for danger, did not come off the turning steel'. He had left it to the man himself to use his own privately made rake to push the coils out of the way. 'It is insufficient and improper to leave it to a skilled man on output bonus earnings to neutralize the hazard. The fact that a skilled man, confident – it might be, overconfident – in his skill and dexterity, was content to believe those qualities could keep him safe does not excuse the employer from his duty to provide proper equipment . . . Workmen should be relieved of the task of continuously having to watch for a hazard such as this if there are available means of relieving them which are neither expensive nor unreasonably interruptive of production.' But the judge also held that the plaintiff should have stopped the machine when he saw the ribbon approaching and for this reason deprived him of one-fifth of his damages.

Piecework

An important factor in the judge's decision is as in the case above the pressure under which the employee is expected to work, contrasted sometimes with the employers' 'more leisurely duty in the Board room' (Baker v. White, 1962). Piecework in particular is recognized as likely to encourage men to behave with less than normal caution, and management must improve its safety precautions accordingly. In Broughton v. Lucas, 1958, certain new precautions for toolsetters were unpopular because they slowed work and reduced bonuses.

The employers were held 75 per cent to blame when a toolsetter was injured through ignoring these precautions, because they had taken no steps by disciplinary insistence or rearrangement of wages or time to make the new precautions more acceptable. As to the division of liability between employer and employee in these various cases, *see* 'Contributory Negligence'.

Now we have considered when a safe system might be necessary, we can go on to the second problem – *who is liable where such precautions undoubtedly are necessary, but the dangers are ignored either by employer or by employee, or both?*

Liability where Employee ignores Safety Precautions

The following four leading cases between them seem to provide the answers. In Woods v. Durable Suites, 1953, the work carried a risk of dermatitis. Management ran a continuous safety campaign with personal warnings and posters drawing employees' attention both to the dangers and to the appropriate precautions, which were provided. Unknown to supervision, the plaintiff, an experienced man, did not observe the precautions fully and contracted dermatitis. His claim for damages was rejected because by their campaign the employers had taken all practicable steps to prevent injury. 'There is no duty at common law to stand over workmen of age and experience' – once precautions such as these have been taken.

The danger in Crookall v. Vickers Armstrong, 1955, was that of silicosis, from sand on a foundry floor. The adequacy or otherwise of dust-extraction plant was not in dispute; the case turned on the use of masks. Suitable masks were in store, and the foundry manager went round from time to time reminding the men of the hazards and of the need to wear masks. But they were not generally worn, because of the unavoidable discomfort. Eventually the plaintiff contracted silicosis. Vickers Armstrong were held to blame, because they had not conducted the kind of diligent campaign illustrated in Woods's case. Theirs had been a 'somewhat half-hearted attempt'. It was up to them to 'encourage and exhort' their workers with 'earnestness and ardour' to understand and guard against the grave risks. Depending on the kind of danger involved, this judgment may be seen to imply safety campaigns with, for example, personal and regular issue of safety equipment. Merely pointing the dangers out, even in the works' rules booklet, or stating in the booklet or elsewhere that observance of safety rules is a condition of employment, may assist supervision before the accident happens, but in itself is scarcely evidence of a safe system once the accident has happened. 'I do not think that one devises a system of work by saying to a workman: "Read the regulations, and do not break them"' (Barcock v. Brighton Corporation, 1949).

The third case is Qualcast v. Haynes, 1959, an appeal to the House of Lords. Here an experienced foundry worker was injured when he spilled molten metal from a ladle on to his feet. He was not wearing safety boots or spats, though these were available. The employers had conducted no safety campaign to get them worn but there was a notice about them, and the worker knew they were there. The firm escaped liability on the ground that they could do nothing more which would in any way alter the man's appreciation of the risk – he knew already of both the danger and precautions. To hold otherwise would, as was said in Smith v. Austin Lifts, 1959, reduce the relationship of employer and employee to that of 'nursemaid and imbecile child', for it would mean that the employer should have told this workman that molten metal was dangerous. The extreme obviousness of this danger explains why the outcome of the case differs from Crookall's, where really only the employers could be expected to appreciate the risks in invisible specks of dust from the sandy floor. The Qualcast ruling was followed in James v. Hepworth, 1967, another foundry case. The management had put up a notice advising men to wear spats, but only a few did so because of strong differences of opinion as to their usefulness. In these circumstances 'the position of the employers was that they should make provision for the spats, inform their employees that they were there, and let the employees make their choice'. Since this had been done, the immigrant plaintiff's inability to read the notice became unimportant, particularly since the employers had no reason to suppose he was illiterate. He had in any case seen and appreciated the use of the spats, and it was for him to ask for them. This conclusion may be compared in passing with the Chief Inspector of Factories' view that 'in dealing with immigrant labour it is particularly necessary to give clear instructions and to make absolutely sure they have been properly interpreted and understood' (1966 Report).

Lastly another House of Lords decision – McWilliams v. Arrol, 1962. A skilled steel-erector was working nearly 100 feet above ground. He was not wearing a safety belt, fell, and was killed. This case differs from the others in that it was subsequently discovered *there were no safety belts available* even if they had been asked for, which they had not. Clearly the skilled man's habitual disregard for his own safety would constitute some degree of contributory negligence, but it would seem surprising if the employers could escape liability altogether when they had failed to take any precautions whatever against such an obvious danger. Their Lordships' reasoning was as follows. Simply to have had safety belts on the site would not have affected this man's mind or the outcome of the case. It would have been necessary to publicize them, either by *forcing* him to wear them – which in the last resort is not practicable, if only because dismissal is the ultimate penalty for disobedience and that leaves the work not done and the same problem with the next man – or by *informing* him of their existence and their desirability.

This latter course would produce a situation like that in Haynes's case, and so the employers were in fact relieved of all liability. The decision seems to be a far-reaching rejection of employers' liabilities, and has been condemned as such, but its effect may possibly be limited to its own special facts. It will be recalled that where there was a similar degree of danger but precautions which *could* usefully have been taken by the employer, he was liable for negligence; Bath v. B.T.C., p. 37.

General Safety Rules

What overall conclusions can we draw from these cases? Although the judges have not attempted to formulate more detailed rules, the decisions seem to be consistent with these four propositions:

(*i*) *The employer must be satisfied that the employee knows the dangers.* The application of this suggested rule clearly depends on the type of danger. If it is self-evident, as in the cases of Haynes and McWilliams, then little or nothing in the way of instruction or warning about it is required. But if it is hidden or not obvious, as in Crookall and Woods, then the employer must exert himself by all appropriate means to persuade the employee of the peril.

(*ii*) *The employer must be satisfied that the employee knows the precautions to meet the dangers.* Again, this must be interpreted according to the particular situation. If the precautions are as self-evident as the dangers – safety belts for work at heights, etc. – the employee should not need a safety campaign to tell him of their usefulness.

(iii) *The precautions must be available.* True, this is not what McWilliams's case decided, but neither did it declare that an employer could confidently rely on his workers' continued indifference to their own safety. Management's case must be weakened if it is seen to take no interest in its employees' well-being. Liability would almost certainly follow if reasonable precautions were eventually asked for, and were not available (Carolan v. Redpath, Brown & Co., 1964).

(iv) *The employee must know the precautions are available.* If he does not, he has that much less incentive to use them, and that much more opportunity for blaming his employer.

These points are offered as safety rules of the widest application. It is emphasized again that their precise meaning depends upon the facts of each case, but that is broadly typical of the common law. On the whole the judges take a realistic view of the difficulties in each particular situation, assessing not only the work and the danger but the skill, experience, age, and wisdom of the individual concerned. Perhaps the most helpful final reminder of the extent to which the employer's duty of care is individualized is a case already referred to – Paris v. Stepney Borough Council, p. 35.

The Employer's Liabilities for his Employees' Wrongful Acts

VICARIOUS LIABILITY

In every case we have looked at so far in this chapter the employee has tried to show fault on the part of his employer. Each one has been decided on the principle of the master's *personal* responsibility for his servants' safety. But as observed earlier, the impersonality of the limited company and the high degree of delegation and specialization which is necessary in industry today makes this a very theoretical standard of responsibility. The real reason for the accident may well be the default of some person or persons lower down the line, acting possibly in some completely unforeseeable way.

This reflection brings us to another extremely important aspect of the law – cases where the negligence of a fellow-employee, equal, superior, or subordinate, can be clearly identified as the cause of injury, and where there is no evidence of an unsafe system or any other direct failing on the employer's part.

In such cases the law none the less holds the employer liable to the injured person. **By the doctrine of vicarious liability** ('liability in the place of another', or 'liability at second hand') **the common law makes the employer pay for the faults of his employees, even though he personally might have been quite unable to do anything to prevent the accident.** In this respect the rules which follow are entirely different from those we have just considered. *The question is not now 'was the employer negligent?' but 'was his employee negligent?'* The two types of case may overlap, but the rules are still distinct and may produce different answers to particular problems. This point has already been referred to on p. 43 as regards liability for practical jokes and other misconduct.

The employer's absolute liability can be justified on the general principle that 'I am liable for what is done for me and under my orders by the men I employ . . . and the reason is this, that by employing them I set the whole thing in motion' (Duncan v. Findlater, 1839). The rule is also socially desirable, for the sake of the injured person. He is given a claim for compensation which is alternative to his claim against the employee who injured him, and, since the employer is so much more likely to have the money or to be insured, it is a considerably more useful one. At the same time, the rule is not intended to relieve the original wrongdoer of all responsibility. If the injured party successfully sues the master, the master can in turn sue the servant to recover his losses (Lister v. Romford Storage, 1957; Harvey v. O'Dell, 1958) or may summarily dismiss the servant if the act which caused injury was a breach of the contract of employment.

It should be remembered that the injured person may be either another employee or a complete stranger to the firm (e.g. a pedestrian run down by a lorry driver). The right of the stranger to sue the employer has been recognized for many years, but the injured fellow-employee's right is of more recent origin. It was given by the **Law Reform (Personal Injuries) Act, 1948.** This Act abolished the old judge-made rule of 'common employment', whereby employees were presumed to have agreed to run the risks of each other's carelessness, and it also made void any attempt in a contract of employment to limit this extension of employers' liability.

Vicarious liability does indeed impose a very wide range of liability upon the employer. In particular, in so far as it gives rights to injured employees, it represents a great extension of the master's duties we have already examined. A very convincing example of the scope of the rule is offered by the simple facts of Lindsay v. Connell, 1951. Here one employee hammering steel negligently struck the hand of the other who held the steel. The master was liable to the injured man. (At the same time it should be remembered that not every error of judgment amounts to negligence, p. 35.)

Liability of Wrongdoer

So far as the law of torts or civil wrongs is concerned, vicarious liability depends upon two fundamental rules. The first is that **the employer is not liable unless the employee who commits the wrongful act could himself be sued for it.** If the employee is not at fault, then management cannot be blamed on his behalf. What constitutes negligence has been considered at length in the earlier part of this chapter, but the point here may be illustrated by an accident caused through skidding. A person injured in this way would not necessarily have a claim against either the driver or the driver's employer. A skid may be unavoidable (and so not wrongful), or it may be the result of bad driving. Which it is depends on the evidence in the particular case. Similarly, the employer would not be held liable for an accident caused by his lorry driver having a sudden and unexpected heart attack or coronary thrombosis; Waugh v. Allen, 1964.

Course of Employment

The second basic rule of employers' vicarious liability is that before it can arise, **the wrongful act must be committed by the employee in the course of his employment.** If he is not acting directly or indirectly on his employer's behalf, there is clearly no reason why the employer should bear any responsibility for him.

Distinction between Contract and Course of Employment

The difficulty in deciding which acts are within the *course* of employment is that they cannot be confined simply to those which are specified in the actual *contract* of employment. Accidents happen largely because the instructions which are given are not carried out properly, and if the doctrine of vicarious liability did not cover such incidents it would be pointless.

Incidental acts. Consequently to make the doctrine meaningful all such acts as are 'normally and reasonably incidental to a man's day's work' – visits to the canteen, collecting wages, etc. – are regarded as within employment although they are very unlikely to be mentioned in the contract. Some incidental acts such as smoking may even be expressly forbidden by the contract in certain circumstances, but may still be within the course of employment; *see* the Century Insurance case, below. Journeys to and from work are, in the absence of any special arrangement with the employer as to transport, outside the course of employment; Young v. Box, 1951; Bradford v. Boston Fisheries, 1959.

Thus the course of employment extends not only to the proper execution of orders and related activities, but also to their *wrongful execution*, in the sense that the employer's work is done carelessly or disobediently or dishonestly, and in this way the injury or loss is caused. *The test of liability therefore is whether the employer has authorized the act itself, not whether he has authorized the way it is carried out.* If the servant's act is not a way of furthering the master's interests, but is essentially a separate enterprise, undertaken primarily for his own or someone else's benefit, it is out of his employment and he alone is responsible to the injured party.

Disobedience and carelessness. There are many examples, not all of which are easily reconcilable. Among the leading cases is Century Insurance v. Northern Ireland Road Transport Board, 1942, where the servant caused an explosion by smoking, despite a prohibition, when unloading petrol. This was held to make his employer liable for the damage because the damage occurred while the servant was carrying out his orders, namely unloading petrol. Similarly where a garage apprentice who was authorized to move cars but not to drive them drove one and injured a fellow-employee, the employer was liable; L.C.C. v. Cattermoles, 1953. When a warehouseman/van driver caused injury by improperly and unnecessarily trying to drive a heavy lorry away from the warehouse door – a task for which he was not qualified – it was held that even this 'exceptionally blameworthy' act was not so 'gross and extreme' as to be outside his course of employment; Kay v. I.T.W., 1967. The employer was liable for injuries caused by the over-zealousness of a porter preventing a passenger from travelling on what the porter believed to be the wrong train; Bayley v. Manchester Railway, 1872. Accidents caused during drivers' departures from acknowledged routes are also within employment, so long as the deviation is not so great as to become another journey altogether. This is essentially a matter of degree. In Williams v. Hemphill, 1966, a journey of some 100 miles was extended to 150 miles, but this was still within the course of employment. *See also* Stallard v. Whiteley, 1960.

On the other hand are such cases as Conway v. Wimpey, 1951, and Kirkby v. N.C.B., 1959, where the expressly prohibited acts of giving lifts to strangers and smoking in a forbidden area were held to be not so much disobedient ways of performing the master's work but acts of a different nature altogether, and so outside the course of employment. Similarly in Rand v. Craig, 1919, the employer escaped liability for damage done by employees when they tipped rubbish on the wrong site in order to make more journeys and earn more money. In these cases – to repeat a point made above – the wording of the contract of employment is important in so far as it can show whether basically the act complained of was authorized. If the act was so authorized, the fact that the contract prohibited a particular way of carrying it out is irrelevant.

Collective disobedience. Where several employees do their work together in a way contrary to instructions, with the result that one or more is injured, liability turns on the nature of the disobedience. If the employees are merely careless, then the employer is vicariously liable to the extent that some of his employees' carelessness can be said to have caused injury to another. This will be offset by the injured party's share of the blame (Owen v. Evans, 1962 – employer held 25 per cent to blame for collective disobedience; Stapley v. Gypsum Mines, 1953; Williams v. Port of Liverpool Stevedoring, 1956). But if employees deliberately combine to reject clear instructions and warnings, and recklessly set about a job in a way which is obviously dangerous, then the employee who is injured is said to have given his full consent to run the risk, and he cannot make his employer liable even in part for the conduct of his workmates; I.C.I. v. Shatwell, 1964; Bolt v. Moss, 1966.

Assaults, etc. Horseplay and such incidental acts as a 'playful pat' are unlikely to be in the course of employment, and so would not make the employer vicariously liable (Smith v. Crossley Bros, 1951; Sidwell v. British Timken, 1962; but *see* p. 43 as to the possible personal liability of the employer in such cases). Assaults by employees are also excluded if they are acts of personal vengeance and not merely misguided attempts to protect the master's interests; Warren v. Henly, 1948; Poland v. Parr, 1927. Purported arrests are likewise usually excluded.

Permitted acts. Vicarious liability, then depends on conduct by which the employee rightly or wrongly fulfils his orders. But if the contract merely *permits* the worker to do certain things which are entirely for his own benefit, the employer is apparently not liable for any resulting injuries. So in Crook v. Derbyshire Stone, 1957, a long-distance lorry driver whose contract authorized him to stop en route for meals was held personally to blame for an accident caused when he crossed the road from his lorry to a café. Had he been crossing, say, to ask the way, he might possibly have remained within the course of his employment. Again, in Hilton v. Burton, 1961, workers were permitted to borrow the firm's van to go for lunch. A fellow-employee was injured through the driver's negligence on the way back to work. Held: the driver alone was to blame. It is perhaps worth noting that the tendency in other countries is to widen the scope of the owner's liability for the driver of his vehicle. In the Australian case of Comino v. Lynch, 1959, the company was liable for injuries caused by a salesman driving his company car home from his club at night, because it was mutually convenient that he should have free use of it at any time so as to save his employer the cost of providing a garage and to enable him to start his rounds each morning from his house.

Financial loss; Employer's Liability in Contract and Crime

All the cases so far mentioned have been examples of the employer's liability for the employee's torts. Most of them resulted in physical injury but financial loss may also give rise to such liability (Hedley Byrne v. Heller, 1963 – a case of loss through negligent advice; but liability here may be expressly excluded when the advice is given). The worker's actions could also make the company liable in contract or even under the criminal law. If the employer authorizes or appears to authorize the employee to make contracts on his behalf, he is bound by them; White v. McGregor, 1961; Powell v. Wontner, 1962.

With regard to crime, the position is more complicated, depending largely on the way the crime is defined by the Act of Parliament which lays it down. Certainly the mere fact that an employee commits a crime while at work does not of itself take him out of his course of employment, as where a lorry driver delivering goods exceeds the speed limit or drives dangerously and causes injury. Usually the result would be that the employee is prosecuted and the employer made liable for damages in any civil claim which may arise. So the company was held liable to the consignor of the goods when his lorry driver stole them in transit; United Africa Co. v. Saka Owoade, 1957. But the offence may be so defined as to impose criminal liability on the employer as well as or even instead of the employee. If there is a breach of the Factories Act, for example, the employer is subject to prosecution even though the real fault may lie with the employee (*see* p. 94). Less rigorous legislation may make the employer criminally liable only if the actions of the servant are those of a responsible person constituting part of management (Magna Plant v. Mitchell, 1966 – no criminal liability on employer for negligence of depot engineer or mechanic in allowing unroadworthy vehicle to be used).

LIABILITY FOR INDEPENDENT CONTRACTORS

One last aspect of vicarious liability should be briefly mentioned. In Chapter 1 the distinction was made between employees and independent contractors. From this it may be recalled that since there is less control over the independent contractor, there is less responsibility for him. In a few exceptional cases, however, the employer of a contractor may incur liability on his behalf. We have seen already that the employer may find it impossible to escape the personal duties cast upon him by the common law, and this remains so whether he purports to delegate his responsibilities to an employee or to an independent contractor. The same is true if duties are imposed upon him by statute, so that if the employer delegates his duty under the Factories Act to fence machinery, he would still be liable to anyone injured even though he has entrusted the task to an outside expert. Finally, if the contractor is required to do work which carries a

INDUSTRIAL LAW

danger to the public at large, e.g. in road mending, his employer is primarily liable for seeing that the work is done safely (Holliday v. National Telephone, 1899; but the employer will not be blamed for incidental negligence by the contractor unrelated to the inherent danger of the enterprise – Penny v. Wimbledon Urban Council, 1899). The Occupiers' Liability Act, 1957, p. 96, is also relevant here in helping to define the liability of persons who engage independent contractors to do work on their premises.

3: The Employer's Statutory Liabilities for Safety, Health, and Welfare

The Factories Act, 1961, Regulations for Dangerous Trades, and other Occupational Statutes

Supplementing the duties imposed upon the employer by the common law (Chapter 2) are the very much more specific obligations laid down by Acts of Parliament.

Types of Employment protected

The vast majority of industrial workers are covered by the Factories Act, 1961. Others are protected by the Mines and Quarries Act, 1954, and employees in commerce by the Offices, Shops, and Railway Premises Act, 1963. These will be referred to in this chapter simply as the Mines Act and the Offices Act. But statutory coverage is not complete since, for example, farm workers receive only limited protection by the Agriculture (Safety, Health, and Welfare Provisions) Act, 1956, and merchant navy men and fishermen have no comparable protection at all. These gaps in the law lend support to the view that there should be a statutory code laying down minimum conditions of safety for all occupations, and a comprehensive revision has in fact been undertaken by the Ministry of Labour. This may lead to the amalgamation at least of the Factories and Offices Acts. The role of the common law should still be remembered. A worker may be injured either in circumstances not covered by the appropriate Act, or in work to which no particular Act refers. In either case he may still have a claim for damages founded on the common law duties which bind all employers.

This chapter is concerned principally with the Factories Act, but mention will be made as appropriate to the Mines and Offices Acts. Extensive reference will also be made to the numerous statutory

INDUSTRIAL LAW

instruments which have been introduced by the Ministry of Labour under powers conferred by the 1961 Act or previous Factories Acts (*see* p. 61 and s. 76, p. 85). These regulations provide codes of safety, health, and welfare applying to a wide variety of trades and industries, and in still more detailed terms than the rules of the 'parent' Factories Act. Although a full statement of their provisions cannot be given in this book, a knowledge of their existence and effect on particular occupations is essential in any review of industrial safety and welfare. The following paragraph summarizes the safety regulations and orders for dangerous trades in force in 1967.

Regulations on Dangerous Trades

Aerated water, 1921; asbestos, 1931; blasting of castings and other articles, 1949; bronzing, 1912, building and construction, 1948, 1961, 1966; celluloid, 1921; cellulose solutions, 1934; chemical works, 1922; chromium plating, 1931; cinematograph film manufacture, 1928, and stripping, 1939; compressed air, 1958; cotton cloth factories, 1929; cotton shuttles, 1952; diving operations, 1960; docks, 1925, 1934, 1959; dry cleaning, 1949; electric accumulators, 1925; electricity, 1908, 1944; vitreous enamelling, 1908; felt hats, 1902; file cutting by hand, 1903; flax and tow, 1906; foundries (parting materials), 1950; grinding of cutlery and edge tools, 1925, 1950, and metals, 1925, 1950; hemp and jute, 1907; hides and skins, 1921; horizontal milling machines, 1928, 1934; horsehair, 1907; india-rubber, 1922, 1955; ionizing radiations, 1961 (several orders); iron and steel foundries, 1953; jute, 1948; kiers, 1938; lead compounds, 1921; lead smelting and manufacture, 1911; locomotives and wagons, 1906; luminizing, 1947; magnesium, 1946; non-ferrous metal foundries, 1962; painting of buildings with lead paints, 1927, and of vehicles with the same, 1926; paints and colours, 1907; patent fuel, 1946; pottery, 1947, 1950; power presses, 1965; refractory materials, 1931; shipbuilding and repairing, 1960, 1961 (several orders); spinning mules, 1905; testing of aircraft engines and accessories, 1952; tinning of metal hollow-ware, etc., 1909; woodworking machinery, 1922, 1945; wool, 1905, 1908; woollen and worsted textiles, 1926; yarn heading, 1907.

Regulations under revision in 1967 concerned woodworking machinery, docks, the asbestos industry, and the protection of eyes. Regulations are proposed for road-vehicle lifting machines, highly

EMPLOYER'S STATUTORY LIABILITIES

inflammable liquids, abrasive wheels, protective footwear in foundries, anthrax-infected materials, ionizing radiations, and carcinogenic substances.

The Factories Act, 1961, is the most recent in a long line of such Acts going back to the beginning of the last century. Many of its provisions restate those in earlier Acts such as that of 1937, and cases on the earlier Acts may therefore remain valid. Its concern is the safety, health, and welfare of the industrial employee. As a general rule, the person made responsible for carrying out its provisions is the factory occupier – the person (or company) in immediate control of the premises. Usually the occupier is also the owner of the premises, but the distinction is important if the premises are occupied on lease, or are in multi-occupation (*see* ss. 120–2). Since the factory occupier is almost always the employer of those working there, the terms occupier and employer will be used interchangeably in this chapter.

Differences between Acts and Common Law

If the employer contravenes this or any of the other protective Acts, he may be faced with both civil and criminal proceedings (whereas under the common law he is almost always subject only to civil liability). The Acts empower the factories, etc., inspectors to prosecute for non-compliance, preferably before injury has been caused. They therefore have a preventive influence which the common law cannot have. They do not expressly confer rights to sue for damages upon injured employees, but such rights are given by the judges. Although both civil and criminal proceedings may follow a particular injury, it should be remembered that the two types of case are different in both purpose – the one to compensate and the other to punish – and burden of proof, and accordingly liability in the one case does not prove liability in the other. Similarly, the fact that the inspector has not prosecuted for use of a particular machine does not prove that the machine is safe from the point of view of civil liability.

Definition of Factory

Before outlining the provisions of the Factories Act, the legal meaning of the word 'factory' must first be examined. The general rule is laid down in s. 175. This states that **a factory is a place where persons are employed in manual labour in any process for or incidental to the**

making, repairing, altering, cleaning, adapting for sale, or demolition of any article. The process must be carried on by way of trade or for gain (with appropriate exceptions for government, local authority, and certain other enterprises), and the employer must have the right of access to and control over the premises. The premises may be in the open air.

'*Manual Labour*'

Strictly speaking, there can hardly be any work which does not involve using one's hands, and which could not therefore be classed as 'manual' and so covered by the Factories Act. But the judges have explained that work is manual if it is done 'primarily' or 'substantially' with the hands rather than primarily with the brain; Bound v. Laurence, 1892; Hoare v. Green, 1907. Thus a dispenser in a chemists' shop has been held not to be a manual worker, whereas a radio and television engineer may be one; Joyce v. Boots, 1951; Stone v. Haygarth, 1966. Again, the presence of only one or two manual workers does not make their place of work a factory if their employment is not the primary or substantial purpose of the place. So in Joyce v. Boots, a porter doing manual work in a chemists' shop was not protected by the Factories Act. On the other hand, in Stone v. Haygarth, where the premises consisted of two rooms, one a shop for television sales and repairs, and the other the workroom in which one man carried out the repair and servicing work, it was held that his employment was a vital part of the enterprise and therefore that his workshop was within the Factories Act. This decision may clearly cause difficulty because of the number and nature of such activities, and it is perhaps worth recording the observations of the Lord Chief Justice when the case was heard in the High Court in 1965. 'I only hope that (my) words . . . will not be treated, as sometimes is done, as having almost the force of a statute. Nothing I have said is intended in any way to make a room behind a shop "a place where persons are engaged in manual labour" merely, for instance, if it is a room to which a shop assistant goes from time to time . . . to test whether a battery he is selling is in proper condition, or . . . an electric bulb is broken or good, or even to do some minor repair by putting on a piece of solder. These are all cases . . . where the person concerned . . . (is) merely on occasions engaged on manual labour incidental to his employment as a shop assistant.' His judgment was affirmed by the

House of Lords in 1966. An incidental point here is that parts of premises may be regarded as separate factories.

The definition also means that if parts of the premises are not directly or indirectly concerned with 'the process', but are used for some different purpose altogether, then they are not within the Act. While premises used for testing or oiling the product are within the Act (Thurogood v. Van Den Berghs, 1951), probably pure research laboratories would not be. Recent cases indicate that administrative and clerical departments are essentially part of the factory (Popper v. Grimsey, 1962; Powley v. Bristol Siddeley, 1965), but they are in any case now substantially covered by the Offices Act. Passages, stairs, yards, cloakrooms, and canteens are part of the factory, though an executives' restaurant has been excluded; Luttman v. I.C.I., 1955; Thomas v. British Thomson-Houston, 1953. Building and repair work within the premises may not be protected by the Act, since they are not among the specified factory processes; Street v. British Electricity, 1952; Walsh v. Allweather Grouting, 1959.

Other Processes within the Act

Section 175 also defines a number of specific processes as factory processes within the Act. These include shipbuilding or repairing or breaking up, work in laundries which are part of larger business or public institutions, premises used for construction or major repair of vehicles (so that some garages may be factories), factory sidings, printing and bookbinding works, film production (excluding the performers), premises where articles are sorted, packed or washed for factory purposes, gasholders over 5,000 cubic feet capacity, and places where animals are slaughtered or kept for slaughter. Work with machinery on *farms* has been held to be outside the Act.

Students using machinery at technical colleges, etc., are not covered by the Act (Weston v. L.C.C., 1941), since they are not strictly 'employed' there, nor have their employers rights of access and control. The education authority's liability at common law is that of the 'reasonably careful parent'.

Definitions of Mines, Offices, etc.

Generally, the Factories Act does not apply to mines and quarries. These are defined in s.180 of the Mines Act, and the relationship of the two Acts is detailed in s. 184. The scope of the Offices Act is defined in its first three sections. It extends to all buildings or parts of buildings used for administrative or clerical work, to retail shops and wholesale premises, and to those where food and drink is sold to the public for immediate consumption. Railway premises within the Act are buildings in the immediate vicinity of the railway, such as stations and signal boxes. This Act's enforcement is largely in the hands of local authorities, but under it factories inspectors now visit local authority offices and offices in factories.

We turn now to consider the provisions of the Factories Act, with appropriate references to regulations made under it, and to the Mines and Offices Acts.

THE FACTORIES ACT, PART I: HEALTH

The first eleven sections of the Factories Act lay down general conditions of work so far as cleanliness, overcrowding, ventilation, temperature, and the like are concerned. Most of the rules are stated in broad terms, but there are a number of important details. Nearly all the provisions are subject to modification if the factories inspector certifies that they are inappropriate in particular cases.

Cleanliness

Section 1 requires that 'every factory shall be kept in a clean state' and free from smells arising from drains, toilets or similar 'nuisances'. In particular, dirt and refuse must be removed daily from working areas – benches and floors – and the floors must be washed or swept every week. If failure to do this causes illness, a claim for damages is possible. In some industries, e.g. those involving lead processes, washing down or damping must be done daily, and in wool sorting the floors must also be treated with disinfectant. Walls and ceilings must be washed or cleaned (e.g. by vacuuming, as in the Pottery Regulations) every fourteen months, or some parts of them possibly more often, again as in potteries and in wool sorting. If painted, the premises must be repainted every seven years, or, if not, whitewashed every fourteen months. The washing and painting rule usually does not apply in factories where mechanical power is not used and where fewer than ten people are employed. Blast furnaces, generating stations, saw mills, and a number of other processes have been specifically exempted from the rule.

Overcrowding

Section 2 states that there must be no risk to health through overcrowding. Each person must have at least 400 cubic feet in which to work, though some part of this may be taken up by machinery. Air space more than 14 feet above ground is disregarded. The basic figure of 400 cubic feet is increased for certain processes, notably work on electric accumulators, enamelling of metal and glass, wool sorting, and brass casting. Unless the inspector allows otherwise, a notice must be provided in each workroom stating how many persons may be employed there.

Temperature

Section 3 requires a 'reasonable' temperature to be maintained in each workroom, though not by any method causing harmful fumes. What constitutes a reasonable temperature clearly varies with the type of work and the time of year, and there are only a few more precise rules. Thus where most of the work is done when seated, the temperature must be at least 60° F (16° C). In pottery manufacture, 55° is the minimum and 75° the usual maximum, except in oven work where up to 115° is permitted. In woodworking, 50° is the minimum. Other rules as to temperature relate to cotton, flax, hemp, jute, and wool processes, and to work in compressed air. When temperatures are specified, a thermometer must usually be provided in the workroom.

Ventilation

Fresh air circulating to ventilate the room and carry away fumes and dust is required by s. 4. More specific standards of ventilation are laid down for cotton, indiarubber, and jute processes, and for grinding of metals and tools. *See also* s. 63, and as to laundries, s. 71.

Lighting

Section 5 provides for sufficient and suitable lighting, natural or artificial, in places of work or passage. More details are given in the Factories (Standards of Lighting) Regulations, 1941. The minimum standard of illumination at any place of work is that provided by six foot candles. (This has been criticized as inadequate by modern standards, and the Department of Scientific and Industrial Research has proposed that the minimum standard of light should be equivalent to fifteen candles one foot away from the work.) The regulations require that undue glare and shadow be avoided, and that windows be kept clean – though they may still be whitewashed or shaded. Certain factories are exempted from the minimum standards, such as those where sensitive photographic materials are made or used, gas works, cement works, coke ovens, and various iron and steel processes.

Drainage

Effective drainage must be provided for processes which make the floor wet (s. 6). Regulations on pottery, chromium plating, and other processes restate this rule in more detail. Special provision for draining off petrol is required for aircraft engine testing.

Toilets

Section 7 and the Sanitary Accommodation Regulations, 1938, lay down the minimum standards appropriate to the number of employees (generally, one water closet for every twenty-five employees, but fewer if more than 100 are employed), with rules as to cleanliness and privacy.

Enforcement

Sections 8, 9, and 10 explain the powers of enforcement of the preceding sections which are vested both in local health authorities and in the factories inspectors.

Medical Supervision

The last section in Part 1 of the Act, s. 11, gives the Minister of Labour power to introduce medical supervision, as distinct from treatment, in any factory where conditions of work cause risk to health. No regulations have yet been made under this section, but *see* ss. 62 and 118.

Before leaving this Part, we may note that the Offices Act lays down standards concerning cleanliness, overcrowding, temperature, ventilation, lighting, and toilets which are substantially the same as those in the Factories Act, though the Minister may in some cases grant indefinite exemption from these requirements (ss. 45 and 46). It is perhaps worth observing also that s. 21 of the Offices Act accepts that noise and vibrations may be sources of injury to health, whereas the Factories Act does not mention the problem of noise at all. The

Mines Act has comparable rules as to ventilation, lighting, conveniences, and cleanliness – the latter so far as measures against vermin and insects are concerned.

THE FACTORIES ACT, PART II – SAFETY

Guarding Dangerous Machinery
Sections 12, 13, and 14, lay down very important rules on the fencing of machinery. They are, in short, that **every flywheel and moving part of a 'prime mover' (an engine or motor), every part of transmission machinery (belts, shafts, wheels, pulleys, etc.), and every dangerous part of any other kind of machinery must all be securely fenced, unless they are in such a position or of such construction that they are as safe as if they were securely fenced.** Section 12 is the section dealing with prime movers, and flywheels directly connected to them; s. 13 with transmission machinery, including rules as to use of driving belts and means of cutting off power, and s. 14 with all the remaining unspecified types of machinery which may be regarded as dangerous. Section 14 also states that fixed guards are unnecessary if a device is provided which automatically prevents the operator from coming into contact with the dangerous part. Section 17 of the Offices Act and s. 82 of the Mines Act provide similar rules.

The precise effects of ss. 12, 13, and 14 have been considered over and over again in the courts. A very detailed account of the judgments appears in Redgrave's *Factories Acts*. The main points may be stated as follows:

Which employees are protected. These sections apply to 'every person employed or working on the premises'. They therefore protect not only the man who operates the particular machine, but also anyone else whose job brings him into the factory and exposes him to risk from the machine (Massey Harris-Ferguson v. Piper, 1956; but in Hartley v. Mayoh, 1954, a fireman called in during an emergency was held to be outside the scope of the Act).

Machinery within the Act. Not all types of machinery in the factory are affected; only those which are part of the equipment of the factory, i.e. used in or incidentally to the factory 'process'. For this reason machinery which is made or tested in the factory in order to be sold is not covered; Parvin v. Morton Machine, 1952. But machinery being run through before actual use in the factory is within the Act. In Quintas v. National Smelting, 1961, it was held that an overhead travelling cable-way and the buckets it carried were not all one piece of machinery, and that it was therefore unnecessary to fence it all – or even at the one point where there was a likely risk. But where a mobile revolving crane was used in the course of factory work this was classed as machinery within the Act and the employers were liable for leaving the 'nip' between the crane and its wheels unfenced (Liptrot v. British Railways Board, 1967 – in which the Quintas decision was criticized in passing).

Purpose of fencing. The judges have interpreted the fencing regulations so that they apply to one only of the possible risks of work on machinery. They have decided that *the purpose of the fencing is that it should keep the worker out of the machinery*, and conversely that if injury occurs because of machinery breaking and flying out at the worker, or from the product in or on the machine, the Act does not apply.

This very important limitation on the scope of the Act was settled in a number of leading cases. Nicholls v. Austin, 1946, decided that there was no liability for failure to fence a circular saw in such a way as to prevent a piece of wood from being ejected. This was followed in Close v. Steel Co. of Wales, 1961, in which the employer was held not liable to a workman who was injured when the bit of his electric drill shattered. Similarly, where a man was injured by the sudden unexpected movement in the machine of a bolt which he had just milled, he had no claim, because he was injured by the *product* and not on the machine itself; Eaves v. Morris Motors, 1961. Nor did the injured employee have a claim for breach of the Act where the injury to his hand came about originally by contact between a hand tool and the machinery, i.e. not through the *personal* contact with it which the judges say is the only incident the Act is intended to prevent; Sparrow v. Fairey Aviation, 1962. On the other hand, fencing *is* necessary against dangers arising on otherwise safe machinery at the point of contact between the product and the machine (Midland Iron and Steel v. Cross, 1965 – liability for failing to fence the 'nips' between metal rods and the rollers into which they were being handfed). It is also possible that injuries in the circumstances which are not covered by the Act may give rise to successful common law claims, but that would depend on whether the injuries were reasonably foreseeable. There was, for example, no alternative liability at common law in Nicholls v. Austin or in Eaves v. Morris Motors, because the injuries were regarded as unpredictable. But in Kilgollan v. Cooke 1956, where the injury was caused through strands of wire breaking and flying out as they were drawn round the machine, the evidence showed that breakage and minor injuries were common occurrences, and so the employer was liable for having unsafe equipment (*see* p. 39).

These various subtleties have considerably reduced the apparent protection given by the Act, and have been widely criticized. A judge in the Court of Appeal said in Eaves's case that the question of protection was now 'technical and artificial' and the protection itself 'illusory'. He concluded: 'There is no protection under s. 14 against a class of obvious perils caused by dangerous machinery, namely, perils which arise from a dangerous machine ejecting at the worker pieces of the machinery itself. Thus, there is now left a gap which neither logic nor common sense appears to justify.' Whether the judges will feel free to change their own interpretation of the words of the Act, or whether a new Act is required, remains to be seen.

Definitions of dangerous machinery and secure fencing. Some of the difficulties in applying ss. 12, 13, and 14 arise from the fact that the words 'dangerous' and 'secure' are essentially matters of opinion. The judges have attempted to define them by saying that *a part of a machine is dangerous if it is a reasonably foreseeable cause of harm*, and that *a guard is 'secure' if it prevents such reasonably foreseeable injury*. Since the standard is that of *prevention,* and not simply of reducing the risk, it follows that machinery may have to be so completely guarded as to make it for all practical purposes useless. This was the decision of the House of Lords in Summers v. Frost, 1955, where the employer was found liable to an employee injured on a grindstone despite the fact that it was fenced so far as was practicable. This contradiction between law and practice can be overcome by means of statutory instruments (*see* p. 59), which may limit the general terms of the Act in particular cases. The Woodworking Machinery Regulations, for example, require only such fencing as is practicable. But there are still no regulations on fencing grindstones, or other types of machine affected by similar rulings on strict liability (*see* Davies v. Owen, 1919 – calendering machine; Sowter v. Steel Barrel Co., 1935 – power press; Dennistoun v. Greenhill, 1944 – cutting machine; Mackay v. Ailsa Co., 1945 – drilling machine).

Foreseeable harm. Since the above definitions of the words 'dangerous' and 'secure' turn on what is reasonably foreseeable, it follows that *the Act, like the common law, requires the employer to predict the likely behaviour both of his machinery and of employees working on or near it.* Thus the unexpected action of the machine was one of the reasons why Eaves lost his claim for breach of statutory duty, and similarly in the cases of Nicholls and Close, above. As might be expected, however, deciding upon the sort of *human* behaviour which is reasonably foreseeable, and which must therefore be guarded against, has caused even more difficulty. The rule is expressed in Mitchell v. North British Rubber Co., 1945. The judge said that a machine is 'dangerous' if 'in the ordinary course of human affairs danger may reasonably be anticipated from its use unfenced, not only to the prudent, alert, and skilled operative intent upon his task, but also to the careless and inattentive worker whose inadvertent or indolent conduct may expose him to risk of injury or death from the unguarded part'. Some degree of foolish behaviour, in other words, is reasonably foreseeable, and to that extent the employer must guard the employee against the consequences of his own folly (Wraith v. Flexile Metal, 1943). The principal effect of the rule which should be noted here is that although the employer's statutory liability is stated in strict or 'absolute' terms, it may still be reduced or even eliminated by the particular circumstances of the injury. To refer back to 'Definitions' (p. 69), for example, it was held in Ward v. Castings, 1962 (a county court decision) that the employers were only two-thirds to blame for injuries received by a worker which were partly due to his own careless use of a grindstone – which, according to Summer v. Frost, should in any case have been completely enclosed, but, of course, was not. Where exactly the line is drawn, and how far liability can be measured in percentages of blame on each side, is dealt with more fully under 'Contributory Negligence', pp. 104–9.

Position or construction of machinery. As an alternative to fencing the machinery, the employer may be able to show that it is equally safe through its 'position or construction'. This involves more than proving that the machinery is beyond arm's reach, or accessible only by ladder, or that it does not normally have people working at or near it. If an employee could be expected to come into contact with it (even when doing something he was not authorized to do – Uddin v. Associated Portland Cement, 1965), then it must be fenced.

Other Rules

Mention has already been made of the way the Act's provisions on dangerous machinery are modified by, for example, the Woodworking Machinery Regulations. It is convenient to note here that other regulations enlarge upon the basic precautions in a variety of ways. Those concerning the production of jute, for example, list in detail the particular kinds of guards required for different machines in the process. There are elaborate rules on safety of electricity generating machinery, covering its insulation, the construction of switches, fuses, switchboards, earthing, and so on. The Power Presses Regulations lay down stringent precautions requiring among other matters thorough examination and testing of presses when first installed in the factory, six-monthly or yearly tests thereafter, and tests of safety devices after every four hours of use.

Work on Unfenced Machinery

Sections 15 and 16 (and similar rules in the Offices and Mines Acts) supplement the last sections by stating that guards on machinery must be soundly constructed, properly maintained, and, with the following strict exceptions, kept in position while the machinery is in motion. Where *examination, lubrication, or adjustment* is immediately necessary, trained and certified machinery attendants who must be over 18 and wearing prescribed safety overalls may work on unfenced moving machinery. These requirements, set out in detail in the Operations at Unfenced Machinery Regulations, 1938, are very strictly applied. Tool setters are not in their own right machinery attendants, and so must be certificated in accordance with these regulations; Nash v. High Duty Alloys, 1947. They are, however, free from the rule as to overalls. Problems have arisen as to when a machine is 'in motion' for the purpose of these sections. In Richard Thomas and Baldwins v. Cummings, 1955, it was held that a machine being moved by hand was not 'in motion' in the sense contemplated by the Act, and therefore could be worked at unfenced by someone who was not a machinery attendant without consequent liability for injury upon the employer. A machine moved at a very slow speed by means of an inching button is also regarded as not 'in motion'; Knight v. Leamington Spa Courier, 1961. But when the machine is going at a high speed, for however short a time, it is in motion and so must be fenced; Stanbrook v. Waterlow, 1964.

Sale or Hire of Machinery; Fencing of Pits, etc.

Section 17 requires sellers or hirers of machinery for use in factories in the United Kingdom to ensure that certain dangerous parts of the machinery, notably shafts and wheels with projecting bolts or set-screws, and toothed or friction gearing, shall be safely constructed at the time of sale or hire. The seller or hirer may be fined if he does not comply with this section, but illogically he is under no statutory liability in damages to anyone injured by his non-compliance; Biddle v. Truvox, 1951. Section 18 requires the fencing or covering of fixed vessels or pits containing dangerous substances and also regulates the construction of ladders or gangways in or on such vessels. Section 19 lays down the minimum distance (18 in.) between traversing parts of self-acting machines and other fixed structures.

Work by Young or Unskilled Persons; Fencing of Pits, etc.

Section 20 prohibits women and young persons (males or females under 18) from cleaning dangerous moving machinery, and s. 21 requires that young persons shall work upon certain types of machinery only if they have been fully instructed in the dangers and are either trained or undergoing training in their operation. These machines are specified in the Dangerous Machines (Training of Young Persons) Order, 1954. They include brick and tile presses, milling machines, power presses, and guillotines. Other prohibitions and limitations on the employment of women and young people are referred to under ss. 73–5. Further rules about instruction and training – regardless of age – appear in, for example, the Ionizing Radiations Regulations and the Woodworking Regulations. The Offices Act also regulates the cleaning of dangerous machines and supervision of young persons at work on them, while the Mines Act prohibits unskilled persons from doing any kind of work in mines unless under supervision.

Lifting Equipment

Sections 22–7 of the Factories Act lay down precautions for various different types of lifting equipment – hoists and lifts, chains and ropes and other lifting tackle, and cranes, including overhead travelling cranes. Detailed rules are contained in the Hoists Exemption Order, 1938, the Chains, Ropes, and Lifting Tackle (Register) Order, 1938, and the Cranes and Other Lifting Machines (Register of Examinations) Order, 1938. The general duties are to ensure good construction, sound material, adequate strength, and proper maintenance. These are strictly applied, so that as regards lifts, for example, the employer is liable if a breakdown does occur, despite the most systematic maintenance; Whitehead v. Stott, 1949; Galashiels Gas Co. v. O'Donnell, 1949. His liability may be reduced if the injured employee misused the lift; Blakeley v. C. and H. Clothing 1958. More specific rules refer to testing, regular inspection of lifting tackle at least once every six months and of cranes etc., every fourteen months, marking safe working loads, safe gateways on lifts, efficient safety devices, and the like. Effective warning measures are required for those working near travelling cranes. Further details appear in regulations for particular trades covered by the Act, such as the Construction (Lifting Operations) Regulations, specifying adequate training for crane drivers – which is not required by the Act itself – crane cabins, safe signalling systems, etc. Comparable general rules are stated in the Mines Act. Hoists and lifts regulations like those above have been drafted for application in shops and offices.

Safe Place of Work

The next two sections, 28 and 29, are of great importance, laying down safety rules applying to all parts of the factory. Section 28 states that *all floors, steps, passages, and gangways in the factory must be soundly constructed, properly maintained, and, so far as reasonably practicable, kept free of obstructions and slippery substances.* This rule has been elaborated upon in a number of judgments. 'Floors', for instance, exclude 'mother earth' (Newberry v. Westwood, 1960), and planks laid across the steelwork of a gantry (Tate v. Swan Hunter, 1958), but include the sill round the inside of a dry dock and the sand bed of a foundry (Taylor v. Green, 1951; Harrison v. Metropolitan Vickers, 1954). In Latimer v. A.E.C., 1953, it was held that the main purpose of the section was to ensure that the floors, etc., were *structurally* sound, rather than to make sure there was no irregularity or temporary hazard upon them. But reasonable care must still be taken to see that unnecessary hazards are removed, as below. Since the standard is that of reasonableness, the effect of this part of the rule is the same as the common law, i.e. there is no guarantee of safety. *See* Latimer's case, p. 36.

Obstructions. Another problem raised by s. 28 is as to the meaning of the word 'obstruction'. As was said in Marshall v. Ericsson Telephones, 1964: 'It is a question whether this section . . . should be so construed as to treat as being an obstruction anything that happens to stop for a moment in the place defined for movement and transit.' Here a man had tripped over a trolley towbar hidden under long metal bars on the trolley. The judge observed: 'The evidence shows that (the trolley) had been there just a few minutes. It was waiting to be discharged. At no time can it be said that this had become an idle load, left there unnecessarily and not in the ordinary course of routine of work . . . It was essential to have it there in the ordinary course of business.' For this reason he held that it could not be an obstruction, for otherwise any machine or component on a factory floor would be an obstacle. The definition given in Churchill v. Marx, 1964, was: 'An obstruction is something which had no business to be there, something which ought not reasonably to be there.' Accordingly a heavy mould left in the gangway for testing was not classed as an obstruction in that case, nor were paper reels in a storage area in Pengelley v. Bell, 1964. In Fairfield v. Hall, 1964, the employer had given no instructions to keep a passageway clear, but the employee could not prove any direct connection between that failure and his accident in the passageway. It would seem to follow from this reasoning that instructions need not be given – a rule unlikely to stimulate safety-consciousness.

Further rules in s. 28 relate to the provision of hand rails on one, or if there is particular danger, both sides of staircases in the factory (Kimpton v. Steel Co. of Wales, 1960 – three steps up to a machine not a staircase), the fencing of openings in floors wherever practicable, and the sound construction and proper maintenance of ladders – another strict obligation. Much of s. 28 is reproduced in the Offices Act. The Mines Act states more generally that all buildings on the surface of the mine must be kept in safe condition.

Safe Means of Access

Section 29 supplements s. 28 by requiring that '*so far as is reasonably practicable*' a safe means of access shall be provided to every place at which any person has to work and the place of work itself must, again within reason, be made and kept safe. As in s. 28, the rules are subject to common law standards of reasonableness; no guarantee is imported here of complete safety at one's place of work. Again, the duty does not apply to all parts of the factory, e.g. access to or from the canteen or toilet (Davies v. De Havilland, 1951; Cockaday v. Bristol Siddeley, 1965), which may lead to somewhat artificial and arbitrary distinctions. If it applies, however, this section by its reference to 'any person' protects not only factory employees but also visiting contractors' employees, as in Whincup v. Woodhead, 1951. If the factory occupier is liable to an 'outside' worker under s. 29, he may be able to recoup part or all of his losses from the contractor; Hosking v. De Havilland, 1949. More stringent rules as to safe working places are provided for building and construction work, in which every year some 40–50,000 accidents occur. The regulations cover in detail the safe construction of scaffolds, working platforms, roof work, ladders, etc. For other attempts to meet the dangers of this work, *see* in particular p. 78. The Shipbuilding Regulations contain similar provisions, and other industries and trades such as iron and steel foundries, generation of electricity, and woodworking also have specific rules about 'good housekeeping' and the safety of floor areas generally. The Mines Act states general rules like those in s. 29 except that while s. 29 additionally requires precautions for those who may fall more than 6 ft 6 in. from their place of work, the Mines Act accepts a risk of falling as much as 10 ft without precautions being necessary. More specific measures under the Mines Act (ss. 22–54) refer to the number of outlets, pit head conditions, height and width of travelling roads, refuge holes, and support of roadways at the place of work.

Dangerous Fumes, etc.

Where work is to be done in confined spaces such as tanks, vats or pipes in which there may be dangerous fumes, the precautions laid down in s. 30 must be followed. These refer to the provision and dimensions of a manhole, if one is necessary, and to the use by trained employees of approved and periodically tested breathing apparatus.

A sufficient number of employees must also be trained in artificial respiration. If practicable, employees in this work must wear a rope whose other end is held by someone outside the chamber. If a responsible person can certify that the fumes have been cleared and there is adequate ventilation, the latter provisions do not apply. The Chemical Works Regulations contain more specific rules as to breathing apparatus and life belts. Section 31 of the Act lays down similar precautions to meet the risks of explosive or inflammable dust or gas or other substance. The precautions turn chiefly on the enclosure of the plant, prevention of dust, etc., and exclusion of sources of ignition such as welding or cutting operations until all practicable steps have been taken to eliminate the danger. For other precautions against dust, see s. 63.

Boilers

Sections 32–9 lay down the appropriate precautions for the use of steam boilers, receivers and containers, air receivers, and water sealed gasholders. The rules, supplemented by the Examination of Steam Boilers Regulations, 1964, cover maintenance and testing and provision of safety valves and pressure gauges. They refer, like many other sections, to periodic examination of the equipment by 'a competent person'. The qualifications of this person are not, however, defined anywhere in the Act.

Fire Precautions

The next twelve sections, ss. 40–52, provide a detailed scheme of fire precautions. After a serious fire in 1956 it was found that the precautions laid down in the 1937 Act were widely ignored. The new provisions first appeared in the Factories Act of 1959. The general rule is that the factory occupier must apply to the local fire authority for a certificate, to be given only after examination of the premises, that there is suitable means of escape from the factory. The authority may require alterations to the premises to achieve this. The employer must then keep the escape routes free from obstruction, and notify the authority of any substantial alterations in the use or structure of the factory. A fire warning system audible throughout the factory must be provided, and suitable instruction given. The latter rules do not, however, apply to factories employing fewer than twenty persons, or fewer than ten persons above ground level, unless explosive or highly inflammable materials are used or stored. In all factories the doors must be easily opened from the inside, and, unless they are sliding doors, open outwards. Lifts and hoistways must be enclosed with fire-resistant materials. Doors and windows intended particularly for fire escape use are to be clearly marked, and a clear passageway provided through all workrooms. Fire-fighting equipment must be readily available. Additional rules apply to celluloid manufacturing, chemical works, and a number of other processes. The Offices Act's fire precautions are very similar to those of the Factories Act, while the Mines Act makes appropriate provision for means of escape and rescue, and for other fire hazards in sections governing the use of safety lamps.

Joint Safety Councils?

Section 53 resembles s. 11 in empowering the Minister of Labour to order special safety supervision in factories where the accident rate shows this to be necessary. No orders have been made under this section, but it appears to enable the Minister to compel both the establishment of joint safety councils and the appointment of safety officers. Since despite all the statutory and common law rules – often ignored – the industrial accident figures remain consistently high, such other ways of tackling the problem may usefully be considered. One of the greatest difficulties in accident prevention is that of stimulating safety-consciousness in each individual employer and employee. The evidence is that when joint safety councils are established they are remarkably successful in reducing the accident rate and they are certainly endorsed by the Factories Inspectorate. A detailed discussion appears in J. L. Williams's *Accidents and Ill Health at Work*. At the moment joint councils are voluntary and exist in only about 4,000 factories in Britain out of a possible quarter of a million. But in 1966 the Minister of Labour said that if the voluntary approach to joint consultation was not more successful within a few years, the Government would take compulsory powers. It is interesting to see that the Mines Act already encourages joint action. By s. 123, miners' associations may appoint a panel of people, each with five or more years' practical experience of mining, and the employer must enable two members of the panel, one or both of them employed at the mine, to inspect every part of the mine and its equipment at least once a month. These representatives are entitled to bring in advisers, to inspect official documents, to make and publicize reports, and to visit accident sites.

Another possible solution to the safety problem is illustrated by the Workers' Protection Act which was introduced in Sweden in 1949. This Act compels employees in smaller factories to appoint safety delegates. They are given statutory rights of inspection, and must be consulted by the factories inspector. Where more than fifty persons are employed at a factory, the Swedish Act also requires that a safety committee of employers' and employees' representatives be appointed.

Safety supervisors. As regards safety officers, it is perhaps curious that their appointment is not expressly required by the Factories Act itself for any type of factory, however large it may be or however dangerous the work. It might, of course, be thought undesirable to appear to make safety the responsibility of only one person in the factory. On the other hand, the Mines Act is very much concerned with the appointment of suitably qualified managers and under-managers, surveyors, deputies, and other officials, and with their individual safety responsibilities. By s. 8, for example, 'no mine shall be worked unless daily personal supervision thereover is exercised by the manager'. There are no similar provisions at all in the Factories Act. Under Ministerial regulations for dangerous trades, however, the compulsory appointment of *'safety supervisors'* is not uncommon. Thus the Construction Regulations state that building contractors employing over twenty workmen, and all demolition contractors, must appoint in writing at least one suitably qualified person to advise the contractor on observing the safety rules, to supervise their operation, and generally to promote the safe conduct of the work. The supervisor must not be given other work which would prevent him from fulfilling these duties. The same person or persons may be appointed by several different contractors working on the same group of sites. The Building Regulations require a safety supervisor for scaffolding operations. Other regulations requiring supervisors include those on work in compressed air, ionizing radiations, luminizing, potteries, and shipbuilding.

Returning now to the provisions of the Factories Act itself, the remaining sections of Part II, 54–6, state the powers of magistrates' courts on complaint by an inspector to prohibit or limit the use of any machinery or part of the factory which may be dangerous. The inspector apparently cannot do this by himself in the course of a factory visit, though an inspector of mines has such power (Mines Act, s. 146).

THE FACTORIES ACT, PART III: WELFARE

Drinking and Washing Facilities
By s. 57 there must be a supply of wholesome drinking water marked as such and conveniently accessible to all employees, either from a public main or otherwise renewed daily. Unless the water comes from an upward jet, cups must be provided, with means of rinsing them. Hot drinks must be provided for those working in compressed-air conditions. Section 58 lays down that adequate and suitable washing facilities must be provided and maintained, with clear running hot and cold or warm water, and soap and towels or their equivalent. Failure to comply with the Act led to a successful claim for damages for dermatitis in Reid v. Westfield Paper, 1957. If in other respects the washing facilities are adequate, however, the inspector may grant exemption from that part of the section requiring running water. Many trades are covered by more detailed rules on washing facilities. The Iron and Steel Foundries Regulations provide for shower or other baths, while the chemical works, lead manufacturing, potteries, vitreous enamelling, and other regulations specify the nature and number of units of 'basins and troughs'. Some rules, e.g. as to lead processes, require employees to be given 'washing time'. Regulations on chemical works, and on lead, indiarubber, wool, and yarn processes are among those imposing positive duties on employees to wash their hands and in some cases arms and faces before handling food or leaving the factory. Frequent inspection of employees' hands is required in biscuit factories, chromium plating, dyeing, and tanning work. A worker on lead compounds is obliged to take a bath at least once a week. The Chemical Works Regulations require the employer to keep a bath register containing a list of persons employed on specified processes, and the date on which each one takes a bath. The Mines and Offices Acts have comparable general provisions on the supply of washing facilities and drinking water.

Clothing Accommodation

Section 59, like s. 12 of the Offices Act, requires suitable accommodation to be provided for coats, etc., not worn during working hours and for drying the same. No general standard of suitability has been laid down, e.g. as to the provision of individual lockers, but it has been held that the risk of theft should be taken into account; McCarthy v. Daily Mirror, 1949; Barr v. Cruickshank, 1959. Since the common law imposes no obligation on the employer to protect his employees' belongings from theft it could clearly be important to establish whether goods were stolen from a factory or office, or from some other 'unprotected' place of work; Edwards v. W. Herts Hospital Management, 1957. Regulations restate the clothing accommodation rule in various ways for a large number of trades and industries. The Potteries Regulations, for example, do not allow such accommodation to be provided where meals are taken, nor where dusty processes are carried on. A separate place is required for protective clothing to be worn at work, with separate pegs for each employee. Rules for some trades specify that the accommodation shall be in the charge of a responsible person. The Patent Fuel Manufacture Regulations lay down that the clothing shall be kept 'under lock and key'.

Seats

A number of seats must be provided for employees who may have the opportunity to sit without detriment to their work; s. 60. If the work can properly be done when the employee is seated, suitable seats, with foot-rests if need be, must be provided for each individual. In luminizing work, the seats must be cleaned daily. The general rules stated in s. 60 appear also in the Offices Act.

First Aid

Section 61 and the regulations made under it concern medical treatment in the factory. The basic rule is that one first-aid box must be provided and maintained for every 150 employees, or every fraction of that number. The contents of the box are laid down in detail in the First-Aid Boxes in Factories Order, 1959, and the First-Aid Boxes (Miscellaneous Industries) Order, 1960. The box must be plainly marked, easily accessible, and in the care of a responsible and readily available person who, if there are over fifty employees, must be trained in first-aid treatment (First-Aid (Standard of Training)

Order, 1960). Although in practice these much criticized minimum provisions may often be improved upon, more elaborate arrangements are required by law in only a few industries. Ambulance rooms are necessary at large building sites, blast furnaces, chemical works, clay works, oil cake mills, saw mills, and in shipbuilding. In each of these processes a certain minimum number of persons, generally either 250 or 500, must be employed before the rule applies. The regulations state the contents of the ambulance room and prescribe that it shall be in the charge of a nurse or other suitably qualified person. By these and other trade regulations it may also be necessary either to provide an ambulance, or to appoint someone whose duty it is to summon an ambulance, or, as with work in compressed air, to make advance arrangements with a nearby hospital. The Offices and Mines Acts contain similar general provisions.

Welfare Regulations; Protective Clothing

The Minister of Labour is empowered by s. 62 to make regulations regarding meals, protective clothing, ambulance and first-aid arrangements, seats, rest rooms, and medical supervision of employees in appropriate cases. The rules on medical supervision will be summarized under s. 118, p. 89. The operation of these welfare regulations in a particular factory may depend on an application for them by a majority of employees (as in the provision of shower baths under the Oil Cake Welfare Order, 1929), and employees may share in the management of these arrangements if by a majority they agree to contribute to the cost. No welfare orders at present in force involve shared administration or contributions from employees. The effect of some of the regulations has already been referred to as regards drinking water, washing facilities, and seats. So far as meals are concerned, regulations on building, cement works, chemical works, clay works, glass bottle manufacturing, laundries, lead processes, pottery, sugar factories, wool sorting, and on several other industries state that canteens or other suitable mess-rooms shall be provided. The Offices Act, s. 15, may require the same for shops.

Safety Clothing

Many industries are covered by protective clothing rules made under s. 62. For certain work in iron and steel foundries, gloves, respirators, and goggles are necessary; for abrasive blasting – helmets, gauntlets, and overalls; for pottery work – a variety of overalls, aprons, and head coverings. Similar provision is made as appropriate for aerated water manufacture, asbestos, bronzing, building, cement works, chromium plating, dyeing, electricity generating, enamelling, fruit preserving, glass bevelling, gut-scraping, hollow ware manufacture and galvanizing, jute, laundries, lead processes, luminizing, magnesium, and patent fuel, production of oil cake, sack cleaning and repairing, ship building and repairing, tanning, and tin plating. The rules may say how often the overalls, etc., shall be cleaned or renewed; e.g. in certain chemical processes, daily. It is perhaps relevant here to note that other forms of protective equipment may be required by the regulations, such as safety nets or belts for construction work and barrier cream in patent fuel production. Usually employees are put under strict obligation to use the safety equipment, but the rule as to safety belts for construction work is of special interest in referring only to 'such persons (as) elect to use them' – a crucial point which negatived statutory liability in McWilliams v. Arrol, 1962, p. 49.

THE FACTORIES ACT, PART IV: HEALTH, SAFETY, AND WELFARE (SPECIAL PROVISIONS)

Dust and Fumes

Section 63 of the Act requires that all practicable measures be taken to prevent employees inhaling injurious or offensive dust or fumes, and to prevent substantial quantities of any kind of dust from accumulating and being inhaled in any workroom. Where practicable, exhaust appliances must be installed. Stationary internal combustion engines must not be used in a workroom unless partitioned off and with exhaust escape into the open air.

It will be seen that this section supplements the rules on ventilation in s. 4 and work in confined spaces in s. 30. The chief problem it raises is the meaning of 'practicable'. If, for instance, exhaust appliances cannot be provided (*see* Richards v. Highway Ironfounders, 1955), the only other suitable precaution may be the issue of respirators. 'All practicable measures' would then oblige the employer to do all he could to persuade employees to use this equipment. It may be recalled that in Crookall v. Vickers Armstrong, 1955, p. 48, the firm was liable at common law for its 'half-hearted' effort to see that masks were worn against the risk of silicosis. The firm was also liable under this section of the Factories Act, because in the circumstances of the case it imposed a similar obligation to conduct an all-out safety campaign. On the other hand, *although an employee may be able to prove that his firm's precautions were inadequate, he will not win his claim unless he can also establish that he would probably have used the precautions if they had been available* (Nolan v. Dental Manufacturing Co., 1958, and *see* 'Burden of Proof', p. 101). Other cases show that if the existence of the dust is not known nor its harmful nature appreciated, it is not 'practicable' for the employer to eliminate it. But if the dust is visible, then whether or not it is known to be injurious, 'substantial quantities' of it may still give rise to liability; Gregson v. Hick Hargreaves, 1955. Quantity is to be assessed at the time the dust is given off, not by the amount over a period of time; Nash v. Parkinson Cowan, 1961.

The regulations governing some thirty trades and industries also require precautions to be taken against dust, some specifically requiring respirators to be issued. Building operations, chemical works, metal grinding, foundries, lead processes, pottery manufacturing, and shipbuilding are among those covered. There is comparable provision in the Mines Act.

Meals in Dangerous Trades

Section 64 is also concerned with dust or fumes, but in particular with those given off by lead, arsenic, or other poisonous substances. Employees must not have their meals in any workroom where there is such a hazard, nor remain in the room for rest periods except for the brief intervals allowed in spells of continuous employment (s. 86). The employer must provide a suitable meal room elsewhere in the factory. Similar rules apply to a number of industries covered by regulations, e.g. paint and colour works, potteries, wool, and yarn.

Goggles and Screens

By s. 65 the Minister may order suitable goggles or effective screens to be provided for processes with special risk of injury to the eyes. These processes are specified in the Protection of Eyes Regulations, 1938, and are: dry grinding of metals by hand; turning of non-ferrous metals or cast iron (except precision turning where goggles or a screen would seriously interfere with the work); electrical or oxy-acetylene or other similar welding of metals; cutting off cold rivets or bolts; chipping or scaling boilers or ships' plates; breaking or dressing stone, concrete or slag. Regulations on building, cement works, chemical works, foundries, and patent fuel also require goggles to be issued.

The standard laid down in s. 65 is that of 'suitability' or 'effectiveness'. The judges have decided that the best available goggles must be 'suitable' even though they have defects, e.g. a tendency to mist over; Daniels v. Ford, 1955. They must be capable of fitting properly, though ultimately only the employee himself can ensure that they do so fit; Lloyd v. Evans, 1951; Davidson v. Clayton Aniline, 1957; Baxter v. Carron, 1965. *Goggles are 'provided' within the meaning of the Act when they are close to hand or clear directions are given as to their availability.* In Finch v. Telegraph Construction, 1949, goggles had been removed from the workplace to protect them against misuse, and placed in the foreman's office several yards away. The plaintiff did not know they were there. Held: goggles had not been provided. It should be noted that the rules on goggles are of limited scope, and exclude a large number of dangerous processes. Some further protection may, of course, be given by the common law, as seen on p. 40.

Health Hazards; Excessive Weights

The next sections cover a wide variety of health hazards. Section 66 and the Factories (Cotton Shuttles) Regulations, 1952, limit the use of cotton shuttles which can be threaded by mouth suction. Section 67 prohibits the use of white or yellow phosphorus in match-making. Section 68 regulates conditions of work in artificially humid factories. Hygrometers must be installed, read, and recorded daily, and the maximum limits of humidity stated in the first schedule of the Act complied with. Section 69 empowers the inspector to declare underground rooms unfit for work other than that involved in storage. Section 70 regulates conditions of work in basement bakehouses. Temperature and ventilation in laundries are governed by s. 71. Section 72 states that *no one shall be employed to 'lift, carry or move any load so heavy as to be likely to cause injury to him'*. The Offices Act has the same rule, but the Mines Act only protects women and young persons against the danger. The section does not define an excessive weight but maximum loads are laid down in regulations on jute factories, and on pottery and woollen and worsted textile processes. The latter regulations state the maximum compact load for an adult male as 150 lb, and for an adult female 65 lb. These particular figures do not, of course, provide a final definition of what is or is not an excessive load in all circumstances. An employee injured when lifting a heavy weight may have a claim for damages at common law if he can prove that an unsafe system has been permitted, but *see* p. 45 as to the difficulties involved.

Sections 73–7 prohibit employment of females under 18 in parts of factories where certain glass or salt processes are carried on, and they also prohibit the employment of women or anyone under 18 in specified zinc or lead work, unless, in the case of work on lead compounds, there are efficient exhausts and other precautions. Similar prohibitions or limitations affect women in pottery, textile, and other processes, and young persons in asbestos works, on brick and tile presses, or working with cellulose solutions, or in chemical works, docks, and various other occupations.

Regulations on Dangerous Trades

Section 76 is the important section under which the Minister of Labour may make regulations governing dangerous trades. Many of the existing regulations were made under the powers conferred in similar sections in earlier Factories Acts, e.g. s. 60 of the 1937 Act, and continue in force. The list of regulations now in force appears on p. 60.

Miscellaneous provisions in ss. 77–9 prohibit the import and sale of matches made with white phosphorus; empower the factories inspector to take samples of dangerous or prohibited materials; and require the inspector's approval of plans for cotton cloth factories which are submitted to local authorities.

THE FACTORIES ACT, PART V: NOTIFICATION AND INVESTIGATION OF ACCIDENTS AND INDUSTRIAL DISEASES

Notifiable Accidents

For the inspector's work to be effective, it is necessary for him to know where accidents have occurred. *Section 80 obliges the employer to notify the inspector of factory accidents causing death or preventing an employee from earning his full wages at his normal work for more than three days*. These three days include the day of the accident and possibly days when work would not normally be done, e.g. the weekend, if the worker remains incapable during that time. All such accidents are affected, not merely those caused by machinery or other matters covered by the Act. The notification must be on a prescribed form which requires full details of the occurrence. The Offices Act has similar rules on notification. The Mines Act, however, refers only to notification of death or serious injury. This Act differs from the others also in requiring notices of such accidents to be sent to miners' representatives as well as the inspector, and in ordering the accident site to be left undisturbed for three days or until the inspector and miners' representatives have visited it, if this can be safely done.

A Ministry of Labour comparison between the notifications required under the Factories Act and claims for industrial injuries benefit made in 1964, indicated that at least 30 per cent of accidents were not being reported. The resulting publicity may have been partly responsible for the apparently dramatic increase in the accident rate — from 204,269 in 1963 to 268,648 in 1964. In 1966 the total was 296,610, including 701 deaths. The Chief Inspector's Report for that year, however, found further evidence of non-reporting, estimated at between 17 and 32 per cent of notifiable accidents. The true accident rate can only be guessed at.

Dangerous occurrences

By s. 81 and the Dangerous Occurrences (Notification) Regulations, 1947, *a number of other incidents must also be reported to the inspector, whether or not injury is caused.* These incidents are: the bursting of revolving vessels or wheels; collapse or failure of cranes, hoists, etc.; explosions or fires caused by ignition of dust, gas or celluloid, or by electrical faults, and stopping work for at least five hours; any explosion or fire stopping work for twenty-four hours; explosion of a compressed gas or air receiver. Section 82 requires any doctor whose patient is suffering from an industrial disease to report this to the Inspectorate. The procedure at inquests in case of death by industrial accident or disease is governed by s. 83. Relatives of the deceased and, if appointed in writing, union or other employees' representatives may examine witnesses at the inquest. Section 84 empowers the Minister to hold an inquiry into any accident or disease.

Section 85 lays down the powers and duties of appointed factory doctors.

THE FACTORIES ACT, PART VI: EMPLOYMENT OF WOMEN AND YOUNG PERSONS

Hours of Work

Sections 86–117 deal at length, and subject to numerous exceptions, with the hours of work, liability to overtime and shift work, and rest periods of women and young persons. 'Young persons' are males and females under 18. *The Act makes no reference to the hours of males over 18*, which are matters for negotiation. Section 86 lays down the general conditions, which, subject to overtime and five-day week regulations, are that the maximum number of working hours a week (i.e. excluding meal and rest time) is 48, or 44 for those under 16. Not more than 9 hours' work a day is allowed. The total period of employment in one day – including meals and rest periods – must not exceed 11 hours. It must not start before 7 a.m. nor end after 8 p.m. (6 p.m. if under 16), or on Saturdays 1 p.m. After $4\frac{1}{2}$ hours' continuous employment there must be a break of at least half an hour, but 5 hours may be worked with an interval of at least 10 minutes during that time. Rest periods are, subject to exceptions, to be the same for all employees concerned. By s. 87 the Minister may permit those under 16 to work for 48 hours a week. Work and rest periods must be specified in a factory notice; s. 88.

Overtime

Overtime, which means hours of work exceeding those specified under s. 88, is permitted by s. 89 and subsequent sections. The general rule is that it must not exceed 6 hours a week, nor 100 hours in a year, nor occur in more than 25 weeks in the year. Hours of work per day may then amount to 10, ending by 9 p.m. But if pressure of work so requires, regulations may authorize 11 hours' work a day or 150 hours in the year (100 if under 18). Such regulations apply to a number of food and drink processes and to laundry and other work. Sections 90–6 make the following provisions: the inspector must be notified of overtime arrangements, which must also be recorded in the factory register; employment inside and outside the factory on the same day is restricted; generally employees must not have meals or rests in rooms where work is continuing; Sunday work is, subject to exceptions, prohibited; annual holidays are specified; women in managerial positions are excluded from this Part of the Act; the Minister may suspend the provisions as to hours and holidays in emergency.

Shift Work

Further exceptions to the general rule are made by rules on shift work. By s. 97 the occupier may apply to the Minister to permit shift work for women and young employees. Unless the factory is a new one, a secret vote must then be taken and a majority of employees concerned found to favour the proposal; the Shift System in Factories and Workshops (Consultation of Workpeople) Order, 1936. Shifts must be between 6 a.m. and 10 p.m., or 2 p.m. on Saturday. They may not exceed 8 hours a day, or 10 in a five-day week factory. The Minister may impose conditions as to transport, etc., and, for young employees, opportunities for further education. The permission may be revoked; s. 98. By s. 99, male young persons on certain continuous processes, notably in iron and steel foundries and in glass and paper manufacturing, may work overnight. Maximum hours are again specified, and regular medical examinations required.

In five-day week factories, total daily hours of work may be 10, or 10½ with overtime. But an employer may still employ women and young persons on a sixth day, for not more than 4½ hours and provided there is no other overtime in that week; s. 100.

Miscellaneous Exceptions

Section 101 authorizes work to start at 6 a.m., with Ministry approval. In exceptional processes such as those under s. 99 and in the manufacture of bread, motor vehicle maintenance, and certain work in conjunction with retail premises, hours of work and rest need not be the same for all women and young persons in the factory; s. 102. Sections 103 and 104 make exceptions to the rule that meals and rests may not be taken where work is continued. Where males under 18 are employed with men on continuous processes, the maximum continuous spell of work may be 5 hours; s. 105. The preceding rules as to hours do not apply to young men employed as part of the regular maintenance staff or by a contractor repairing part of the factory or its plants; s. 106. Certain factories, notably those connected with retail trades, may substitute some other day for Saturday as the half-day; s. 107. By s. 108, and regulations made under it in 1947, different sets of employees may take the holidays specified in s. 94 at different times. Section 109 authorizes Jewish-owned factories to employ Jewish workpeople on Sunday. Sections 110–13, and regulations made thereunder, vary the previous rules on hours, meal times, etc., for laundries and food and drink processes. Special health and welfare conditions may be imposed; s. 114. Section 115 requires factory occupiers who wish to use the exceptional provisions laid down by ss. 99–113 to give the inspector at least seven days' notice in writing, and to post the terms of the exception in the factory. The hours of young people employed in carrying goods or delivering messages and in other specified duties are regulated by s. 116. By s.117 the Minister may make further exemptions in the interests of efficiency of industry or transport, but in some cases only on the application of representative bodies of management and labour, or a Wages Council.

Hours of employment in shops are regulated by the Shops Act, 1950. The Offices Act does not provide any rules on this subject for office or other workers covered by that Act. Rules on the employment of women and young persons in connection with mines and quarries are contained in ss. 124–32 of the Mines Act, and are broadly similar to those in the Factories Act. The Mines Act prohibits the employment of females in underground work. Comprehensive restrictions on the employment of persons who are not over school-leaving age are contained in the Employment of Women, Young Persons, and Children Act, 1920.

Medical Supervision

By section 118 and the Young Persons (Certificate of Fitness) Rules, 1948, employment of young persons must be notified to the appointed factory doctor. The doctor must then examine the young person within fourteen days of his or her beginning factory work. Unless a certificate of fitness is given, the employment must be ended (see also s. 92 of the Mines Act). Section 119 empowers the inspector to call for such a certificate.

It is convenient to note here some of the other requirements as to medical supervision in our industrial legislation. Regulations made under s. 99 of the Factories Act provide for six-monthly examinations of males under 18 on night work. A number of trades and processes have differing requirements, not confined to young persons. In lead compound processes, a weekly examination is necessary. For employment in accumulator works, in compressed air, indiarubber processes, lead smelting, luminizing, paint works, and potteries, monthly medicals are laid down. In enamelling, lead processes, tinning, and yarn heading, an examination must be made once every three months, and in patent fuel works and on mule spinning, every six months. The Ionizing Radiations (Sealed Sources) Regulations require medical supervision for all persons whose work involves risk of exposure to radioactive substances, and examination by the factory doctor at least once every fourteen months. Blood tests may be carried out. These regulations also oblige workers to wear radiation dosemeters. In some occupations, a duty is imposed upon the worker to report ailments which may unfit him for work, such as cuts (Wool, etc., Regulations) or earache or colds (Work in Compressed Air Regulations). Exceptional health precautions include limits on the number of hours per week which may be spent on a particular process, and even upon the overall period of employment, as in the Luminizing Regulations.

THE FACTORIES ACT, PART VII: SPECIAL APPLICATIONS AND EXTENSIONS

Sections 120–2 define the liability of the owner of the factory, as distinct from the occupier (*see* p. 61), where parts of the building are occupied by separate factories. Broadly speaking, parts in common use are the responsibility of the owner. The Offices Act is in similar terms. Sections 123–7 extend the operation of appropriate parts of the Factories Act to electrical stations, parts of charitable or reformatory institutions, docks, wharves, quays, warehouses, ships, building operations, and works of engineering construction. Sections 128–32 extend the Act to cover the use of lead paint in painting buildings, and restrict the employment of women and young persons on this work.

THE FACTORIES ACT, PART VIII: HOME WORK

If a factory employer has persons working for him in their homes, as where he distributes materials to them to be made up there, he is bound by ss. 133 and 134 to notify the inspector and the local authority of their names and addresses, and the local authority may prohibit the work if the premises become dangerous to health. The sections apply to a number of trades, largely concerned with furniture and clothing (Homework Orders Variation Order, 1938).

THE FACTORIES ACT, PART IX: WAGES

The Factories Act is not concerned with laying down wage levels or otherwise affecting the processes of collective bargaining. Such laws as there are on minimum wages may be found substantially in the Wages Councils Act, 1959, and the Terms and Conditions of Employment Act, 1959, and, though not strictly speaking law, in the terms of the House of Commons' Fair Wages Resolution, 1946. The Factories Act provides only that pieceworkers in textile factories, shipbuilding, foundries, laundries, sweet making, and other specified processes shall receive such particulars of their rates of pay as enable them to compute what is due to them; s. 135. It expressly prohibits employers from making deductions from wages to pay for any of the safeguards required by the Act. (*See also* s. 144 and the Checkweighing in Various Industries Act, p. 93.)

THE FACTORIES ACT, PART X: NOTICES, RECORDS, ETC.; DUTIES OF PERSONS EMPLOYED

Prescribed Abstract

This Part of the Act contains a variety of obligations upon both employer and employee. By s. 137, a person who intends to use premises as a factory must notify the district inspector at least a month before he does so. Section 138 obliges the employer to put up copies of the 'prescribed abstract' of the Act at the main entrances to the factory. The abstract is a notice prepared by the Ministry, setting out the essential points of the Act. In this way every worker may know what protection the Act gives him – except that the important judgments which explain or modify its effect are not mentioned. There is no similar statement of common law rights. The abstract must include the address of the district inspector so that any employee may contact him if necessary. In 1956 a Government White Paper on the Inspectorate stated: 'Inspectors are instructed to pay attention even to anonymous complaints, and to conduct their enquiries so that no indication is given that a complaint has been received.' Copies of other regulations applying to the factory, e.g. those passed under s. 76, must also be posted; s. 139. It should be noted that some of these regulations in turn provide that safety leaflets must be issued to each employee, e.g. those working on unfenced machinery, or in compressed air, or with lead paint. The Shipbuilding and Ship-Repairing Regulations are unusual in requiring a copy of the regulations to be given to each employee. The Mines and Offices Acts make the standard general provision as to notices, and also envisage personal issue of such information.

General Register; Periodical Returns

Sections 140–1 oblige the factory employer to keep a general register, recording such matters as the number of young persons employed, details of the washing and painting of the factory, accidents and industrial diseases, and variations in the hours of women and young persons. The fire authority's certificate must be attached to the register. The register must be available to the inspector and appointed factory doctor, and be kept for at least two years after the final entry. Where persons are subject to risks from lead poisoning or ionizing radiations and in the case of a number of other dangerous trades the employer must keep a separate health register recording employees' names and, by some regulations, dates and results of medical examinations. Section 142 requires an annual return of the number of employees and other specified particulars.

Employees' Duties

The Act is notable for the number of duties it imposes on factory occupiers. Section 143, however, is a reminder that duties are also cast upon employees, breach of which may be a criminal offence. *An employee must not misuse any appliance or device provided for safety, health or welfare, and where such appliances are provided for personal use, he must use them in the proper fashion. He must not 'wilfully and without reasonable cause do anything likely to endanger himself or others'.* This latter phrase involves some deliberate abuse of the equipment, and not mere handling or mishandling without any such 'perverse' intention. Thus before an employee can be convicted under this section his conduct must be more blameworthy than is usually found in civil contributory negligence cases (*see* p. 104). One such case was Gurney v. Elmore, 1958, where a shop steward was convicted for deliberately doing a job in a very dangerous way, which he had previously joined with management in condemning. It follows that an injured employee may lose part or all of his claim for damages through contributory negligence without necessarily being criminally liable under s. 143, or the equivalent provisions of the Mines or Offices Acts. Prosecutions of employees are in fact rare, averaging less than 1 per cent of the criminal proceedings under the Act. This may well be because it places the primary liability upon the employer and in strict terms which make it difficult for him to take advantage of s. 143 (*see* ss. 155 and 161, p. 94). In building, work in compressed air, chemical works, wool sorting, and other occupations, further obligations are cast on employees – usually to wear the prescribed safety clothing (p. 81), to report defects in plant, or, more exceptionally, not to smoke (aircraft engine testing) or spit (grinding and glazing). Similar duties for health purposes are referred to under ss. 58 and 62.

Checkweighing

The remaining rule in Part X, s. 144, states in effect that weights and measures used for checking wages must be accurate, and may be examined by Board of Trade inspectors. We may note at this point that the Checkweighing in Various Industries Act, 1919, gives employees in iron and steel processes, loading and unloading vessels, chalk and limestone quarrying, and cement and lime manufacturing the right to appoint a checkweigher. His duty is to test the weighing of loads and materials handled or produced in these processes so that payment based on such weights may be accurate. Management must give him all necessary facilities to do this job.

THE FACTORIES ACT, PART XI: ADMINISTRATION

This Part largely concerns the appointment and powers of factory inspectors and other officials. Section 145 enables the Minister to appoint inspectors and requires him to lay an annual report of their activities before Parliament. The Act does not state any positive qualifications for inspectors, but does provide that they must not be factory employers or employees. There are some 500 Factories Act inspectors, who have approximately 250,000 factories to visit. It has been calculated that this ratio permits an adequate inspection of each factory once every four years (and it follows that management and labour must continue to take full responsibility for safe working conditions). Their powers, other than that of prosecuting in the magistrates' courts, are set out in ss. 146 and 147. They have a right of entry during day- or night-time hours of employment into any factory, or into any warehouse where a young person may be employed, a right to see the register and other records required by the Act, and to inspect the premises generally for compliance with the Act. They can examine individuals who are or were within the preceding two months employed at the factory and take signed statements from them, examine medically if so qualified, and 'exercise such other powers as may be necessary'. It is an offence to obstruct the inspector in his duties. Inspectors appointed under the Offices and Mines Acts have comparable powers. The inspector is not obliged to give management advance notice of his arrival, though this is often done. Employees' organizations have no legal right to be consulted or to accompany the inspector on his visit. Such rights are given in some European countries.

Sections 148–54 define the powers of entry of fire authority officers, the appointment and payment of factory doctors, and the medical officer of health's duties. They also provide that the inspector must produce his certificate of appointment if so required by management, and prohibit him from disclosing confidential information other than in the course of duty.

THE FACTORIES ACT, PART XII: OFFENCES, PENALTIES, AND LEGAL PROCEEDINGS

Employers' Criminal Liability

Sections 155–71 state the criminal liability for breaking the Act, and deal with related administrative matters. The duty to see that the Act is complied with is placed primarily upon the factory occupier. If the occupier is a company, any representative of management whose neglect can be shown to have caused the breach may be prosecuted as well as the company, though this is very unusual in practice (s. 155). Only in exceptional circumstances is the company able to escape conviction if a breach occurs. The occupier must show that *'all reasonable steps'* were taken to prevent the incident. So in Wright v. Ford Motor Co., 1966, where injury was caused because a locked guard had just before been forced by an unknown employee, the employer was not guilty. The employer may also be acquitted if he can bring another person before the court as 'the actual offender', but only if he can prove that he himself used 'all due diligence' to enforce the Act, and that the offence was committed 'without his consent, connivance or wilful default'. If at the time of the offence the inspector finds all these requirements are fulfilled, and that the offence was committed against orders, he may prosecute the actual offender and not the employer (s. 161).

Comparison with civil liability. If a breach occurs it is, of course, very difficult for the employer to prove positively that he has taken such a high standard of care, even despite the provisions of s. 143. The Mines Act, s. 157, offers the additional defence of 'impracticability' to mine managers, but this is not open to the factory occupier. An employer may therefore be prosecuted and convicted for the actions of an employee which by the less rigorous standards of the civil law would be regarded as the fault of that employee. In Dunn v. Birds Eye Food, 1959, a labourer in defiance of his instructions left unfenced machinery in motion when cleaning it, simply to save himself the trouble of going to the switch and turning it off. It was held that the resulting accident was the injured man's own fault, but the employer was none the less convicted for the original failure to fence the machine. If the labourer had claimed damages on these facts, he would probably have lost the greater part of his claim through his own contributory negligence. *See* p. 108 and Ginty v. Belmont, 1959.

Fines

The magistrates' court has power to fine the occupier up to £300 for breaches likely to cause death or bodily injury (the penalty is the same in the Offices Act, but in the Mines Act it is £200 and/or three months' imprisonment), and for other contraventions £60, or £15 a day if continued. If an employee is prosecuted, the maximum is £75 (s. 156). While civil claims for damages far exceeding these amounts may also be made, it may still be thought that the penalties upon employers are small in comparison to the possible injury. The average fine upon a company for breach of safety duties is in fact some £50. The court has power to imprison only for impersonation of an inspector, forgery of certificates, and other false declarations (s. 159).

Other court powers include that of ordering the cause of the contravention to be remedied (s. 157) and of fining parents up to £10 for allowing their children under 18 to be employed contrary to ss. 86–119. Section 163 declares that an owner or hirer of a machine in a factory who is not the factory occupier (but is, e.g. a visiting contractor) is liable to his own employees; Whalley v. Briggs, 1954. Remaining provisions in this part relate to appeals, evidence, offences regarding employment of children, service of summonses, and apportionment of expenses between occupiers and owners of factories.

THE FACTORIES ACT, PART XIII: APPLICATION

Sections 172–4 concern the application of the Act to Crown factories, and its application to premises which may be covered by the Mines and Quarries Act.

THE FACTORIES ACT, PART XIV: INTERPRETATION AND GENERAL

Section 175 provides the definition of the word 'factory', stated in detail on p. 61. Section 176 defines a number of other terms used in the Act, ranging from 'bakehouse' to 'young person'. Section 177 authorizes the Minister to promote safety, health, and welfare in factories by research and publicity. The remaining sections, 178–85, concern the making and passing of statutory instruments and orders under the Act, and other administrative matters. The Act ends with seven Schedules. These contain a table of humidity (s. 68); provisions as to factories occupying parts of buildings (ss. 40–8, 52, and 120); powers to prescribe standards (ss. 3–5, 7, 58, and 59); procedure for making special regulations, including publicity and the form of objections; district council powers still operative under the Factory and Workshop Act, 1901, including a prohibition of employment of women within four weeks of childbirth; transitional provisions, and a list of Factories Acts and other statutes repealed by the 1961 Act.

The Occupiers' Liability Act

The occupier of land or buildings has responsibilities for the safety of his premises to anyone who comes lawfully upon them. Usually the occupier is the person in immediate control, but when several people have rights over the same premises which of them is the occupier for any particular purpose depends on the degree of control each exercises. A person who 'lives in' as a condition of employment, for example, may only be liable for his own property on his own part of the premises; Wheat v. Lacon, 1966. Generally, however, the employer is also the occupier and as such is liable for the safety of his factory or office not only to his own employees in the ways we have seen, but also to visiting contractors, commercial representatives, etc. Occasionally his duty towards them is as high as if they were his own employees. He may, for example, exert so much control over their work at the factory that for safety purposes they are regarded as his employees; Garrard v. Southey, p. 5. Again, the Factories Act may expressly make the occupier liable to other employers' workmen on the premises (p. 75). The rules of vicarious liability can produce the same high degree of liability. But usually his responsibilities are less rigorous, for the very reason that the visitors are not his employees. The duty he is then under is laid down by the **Occupiers' Liability Act, 1957.**

DUTY TO VISITORS

This Act greatly simplified the previous common law rulings, which made the occupier's duty vary with the status of the visitor – invitee, licensee, etc. Now, the occupier owes the same duty to all lawful entrants upon the premises, namely to **take reasonable care that the premises will be reasonably safe for the agreed purposes of the visit** (section 2). This duty is in fact less strict than that owed by employer to employee, although the wording is similar. The Act modifies the duty by stating, for example, that it may be restricted or even excluded 'by agreement or otherwise'. It might therefore be sufficient for the purposes of the Act to put up a warning notice of a danger, if the danger could be avoided in this way, whereas between master and servant the hazard itself might have to be eliminated. Again, *the occupier is entitled by the Act to assume that the visitor will guard against the normal hazards of his own trade* when he comes to work on the occupier's premises. So in Roles v. Nathan, 1963, the occupier was not liable to a sweep poisoned by dangerous fumes in the chimney. Similarly in Christmas v. General Cleaning Contractors, p. 38, where a window-cleaner fell because the window sash he was holding on to was loose, this was regarded as a typical hazard of the work which his employer ought to have guarded him against, and therefore the occupiers of the building were not liable for the condition of the window.

If the risk is not an 'occupational hazard' but is peculiar to the premises in question, such as an unusually slippery floor or a defective ladder lent by the occupier, then the occupier will be liable if he knows or ought to know of the danger and has failed to warn the visitor; Crawford v. Allison, 1961. Sometimes, as in Smith v. Austin Lifts, p. 39, the liability is divided between the occupier and the visitor's own employer, if the latter also knew of the risk to his servant and failed to take any steps to reduce it.

Traps

The occupier's duty therefore is to give adequate warning of or other protection against dangers which are or ought to be known to him, but are hidden from the visitor – 'traps', as they are sometimes called. A mat on a highly polished floor is probably not such a hidden danger, but a very slippery floor itself may be. A steep staircase is not likely to be a trap, but the question of lighting may be important. Packing cases stacked 3 or 4 ft high in a public part of a shop were not regarded as a trap in Doherty v. London Co-operative, 1966. But vegetable or other such matter on a shop floor might not be noticeable to a customer, and the occupier could be liable if he did not have an adequate maintenance system; Turning v. Arding and Hobbs, 1949. In another case, the occupiers of a shop were liable for injury caused by a loose brass strip round an inset floor mat. It should be noted that even if the visitor can be shown to be aware of the risks, that fact alone does not prove he has consented to run them, though his conduct in the circumstances may provide evidence of contributory negligence. But *see* Farr v. Butters, below.

Contractors

If the dangers are caused by contractors working on the occupier's premises, the Act states that the occupier is not liable if he has taken reasonable care to see that the premises are safe, e.g. by appointing a competent electrician to install wiring; Green v. Fibreglass, 1958. The contractor himself is then responsible to another visitor injured by his bad workmanship (O'Connor v. Swan and Edgar, 1963 – contractor liable when ceiling under repair fell and injured shopper). But if the person injured by the contractor is the occupier's own employee, it seems that the occupier may still be liable; Sumner v. Henderson, p. 41. An occupier may be liable if visitors' possessions are stolen, if he can be proved negligent; Davis v. Educated Fish Parlours, 1966.

Trespassers and Children

The occupier's responsibility extends only to making the premises reasonably safe for the agreed purposes of the visit. If the visitor strays outside the 'area of invitation', e.g. by entering private parts of the premises, no claim arises; Hillen v. I.C.I., 1934. Towards persons who come on to the premises as trespassers the occupier has no duty of care, except that he must not conduct dangerous operations so as to expose them deliberately or recklessly to risk of injury; Commissioner for Railways v. Quinlan, 1964. But tolerance of child trespassers may bring the children into the category of lawful visitors and so give rise to liability if they are injured, or cause injury to others; Hilder v. Associated Portland Cement, 1962. The occupier should take all reasonable steps to show that the land is private, and so far as practicable maintain fencing or other such precautions; Aldrich v. Boyer, 1960.

OWNER'S LIABILITY FOR EQUIPMENT

The rights of a person who uses equipment owned by another, but who is not the employee of the owner, are broadly similar to those of a visitor on another's premises. Some but not all types of equipment are indeed covered by the Occupiers' Liability Act, which (section 1) refers to the duties of anyone 'occupying or having control over any fixed or movable structure', including vehicles. Whether the Act applies or not, the duty of the owner seems to be primarily to warn the user against hidden dangers. If examination by the user can reasonably be expected, and if the user is free to accept or reject the equipment, then the owner may raise the defence of consent (p. 109) if the user is in fact injured. So in Farr v. Butters, 1932, a man assembling a crane supplied by a contractor noticed a defective part in it, but continued to assemble it and then used it. He lost his claim for damages when injured because of the defect. But where the user had no choice in the method of unloading insecurely stacked equipment, he won. In Field v. Jeavons, 1965, an electrician visiting a factory to wire-up equipment switched on and was injured by a moveable electrical saw which the occupiers had left unsecured. The occupiers were held liable to him to the extent of 75 per cent because although he was not their employee they should still have anticipated that he might switch on the saw to test his work. He lost 25 per cent of his claim because he should have asked permission to switch on.

The owner of the equipment must also exercise a high degree of care to protect against hidden dangers where the user has to rely on the owner's skill or experience in selecting the equipment, e.g. where he provides the scaffolding which others are to use. If dangerous appliances such as acids, explosives or inflammable materials are used, the duty may involve safe packing, or ensuring delivery into safe custody (Philco v. Spurling, 1949; delivery of inflammable scrap to wrong address – deliverer liable; Samways v. Westgate, 1962 – firm liable to injured dustman for leaving carton of rubbish with large piece of glass sticking through the side).

4: The Employer's Defences; Damages and Industrial Injuries Insurance

This last chapter on industrial law concerns two distinct issues. First, the grounds on which an employer can resist a claim for damages for injuries at work, and second, the purpose and assessment of such damages and of the payments provided by the State.

The previous two chapters have indicated in passing the nature of the employer's defences. It may be helpful to describe them here more explicitly, and in particular to make the point that since common law and statutory duties often differ, the defences do not all apply to the two different types of claim.

BURDEN OF PROOF

A rule of general application is that *the injured employee must first prove that the employer's alleged negligence or breach of statutory duty was the direct and principal cause of his injury.* He may succeed in part if he can prove that it was one such cause, but will lose altogether if his own conduct is thought to be the real cause of his injury. In Bonnington Castings v. Wardlaw, 1956, the House of Lords held that it was not enough to establish a breach of duty and merely a *possibility* that the injury was caused in that way. So in Nolan v. Dental Manufacturing, 1958, the employers escaped liability for not providing goggles because the plaintiff failed to prove that he would have worn them even if they had been provided. Simmonds v. Walsall Conduits, 1962, p. 107 and Fairfield v. Hall, 1964, p. 74, are similar cases. On the other hand, where the employee's attitude to safety precautions is not involved, proof of a breach of duty and an otherwise inexplicable injury or disease will be sufficient to make the employer liable (Nicholson v. Atlas Steel, 1957 – inadequate ventilation in foundry – pneumoconiosis – employer liable).

101

Defences

REASONABLE CARE

The employer has a complete defence to claims for damages for failure to provide safe premises, equipment, fellow-employees, or system of work – his common law duties as such – if he can prove he took reasonable care in trying to provide them. This is the standard usually required by the common law, as illustrated in Chapter 2, but it is not necessarily sufficient in other contexts. In vicarious liability claims, for example, it is irrelevant, for it is the negligence of the employee who caused the accident which is in dispute, not that of the employer. Under the Acts of Parliament we have considered, reasonable care is only occasionally expressly made a defence, as in ss. 28 and 29 of the Factories Act. Some sections of the Acts are interpreted very strictly as containing absolute obligations or prohibitions, and if they are not complied with in every respect the employer is liable regardless of the care he may have taken (e.g. s. 22 of the Factories Act). Others use the standard of reasonableness indirectly, in that although the phrase is not stated in particular rules the judges employ the test of 'reasonable foresight' to limit their scope, as with ss. 12, 13, and 14 of the Act (p. 69).

ACT OF GOD

The phrase 'Act of God' should be mentioned here in passing, since it is often misunderstood. In law it has the very limited meaning of an occurrence altogether beyond man's normal expectation or control. In that sense it occasionally operates as a defence in its own right, but basically the issue is still one of defining foreseeable risks and the appropriate reasonable care.

REMOTENESS OF DAMAGE

As noted on p. 34, liability will only be imposed where the injury in question is both a direct and a reasonably foreseeable consequence of the negligence or breach of statutory duty. If one of these factors is absent the law regards the injury as 'too remote' from the original act. This is in effect an aspect of reasonable care, above, but the present point may help to explain that phrase more fully. 'It does not seem consonant with current ideas of justice or morality that for an act of negligence however slight which results in some trivial foreseeable damage, the actor should be liable for all consequences, however unforeseeable and however grave, so long as they can be said to be "direct"' (Overseas Tankship v. Morts Dock (The Wagon Mound), 1961; Doughty v. Turner, p. 34). Reasonable likelihood remains the crucial test. But the injury itself need not be precisely predictable, so long as it is still a likely result of the negligent act (Baker v. Hopkins, 1959 – employer liable for death of doctor called in to help employees trapped through employer's negligence; Chadwick v. British Railways, 1967 – train crash through negligence of B.R. – B.R. liable for nervous shock to rescuer).

'Likely' events may also include foolish, unauthorized or even wrongful acts of third parties (Philco v. Spurling, 1949; Davies v. Liverpool Corporation, 1949 – passenger pressed bell when conductor absent from platform – corporation vicariously liable for resulting injury). On the other hand, it is both a direct and likely result of an accident that dependents may sustain grief and loss, but grief is not and loss may not be compensatable (McDonnell v. Stevens, 1967 – husband had no claim for loss of earnings while looking after injured wife). Again an employer cannot usually recoup his losses when a third party injures his employee; Inland Revenue Commissioners v. Hambrook, 1956. The limits of liability are thus somewhat arbitrary – perhaps unavoidably so under the present system.

DELEGATION

At Common Law
Sumner v. Henderson (p. 41) and other cases emphasize that *the employer's common law liability is personal to him. Generally, therefore, he cannot escape his obligations by delegating their performance to someone else.* Yet as we have seen in Davie v. New Nerton Mills, pp. 40–1, the requirements of reasonable care may sometimes amount to delegation. Similarly in Williams v. Trim Rock Quarries, 1965, where a tool company was demonstrating a drilling machine at a quarry, the judge said: 'The quarry owners recognized that it was their duty to see that their men were properly instructed and warned of the dangers to avoid with a machine like this, but of course they could delegate their duty; and they said, with justice, that in this case it was reasonable for them to leave the instructions to Mr Briggs of

the tool company.' The quarry owners were held not liable for the death of an employee through the machine overturning, responsibility for which was put upon the tool company. These decisions make it difficult to forecast which rule on delegation will be followed.

By Statute

The practice of and indeed the necessity for delegation is, however, clearly recognized under certain statutory provisions. Under the Mines and Quarries Act, for example, the owner is required to delegate various responsibilities to the officials he must appoint. Numerous regulations require the appointment of safety supervisors (*see* p. 78). But *delegation will only be accepted as a defence if the employer can prove that he had clearly and expressly told the plaintiff that the statutory responsibilities were thenceforth upon him*. The employee must in effect be appointed the employer's agent for carrying out the duties; Beal v. Gomme, 1949. This means more than merely telling the employee how to do the job; Manwaring v. Billington, 1952. In Johnson v. Croggon, 1954, builders gave the task of selecting equipment to the foreman in charge of the job. He borrowed a ladder, which broke as he used it. It was held that he, as the person to whom the whole task was delegated, had no claim for his own failure to select properly. Since the defence of delegation only applies where the injured person is himself the delegate, such decisions may be equally well interpreted as examples of contributory negligence, below. Finally, we should note that the protective Acts of Parliament do not permit delegation on all matters. In particular, as seen on p. 67, the duty to fence dangerous machinery is imposed inescapably on the employer.

The three defences outlined above are all aspects of the standards imposed by the law on employers. We turn now to examine what the law demands of employees, and how their own behaviour may affect their claims for damages.

CONTRIBUTORY NEGLIGENCE

The most usual way in which employees reduce their chances of a successful claim is by contributory negligence, that is, by carelessness or indifference to personal risk. The basic rule is that while the duty of avoiding accidents is placed by both common law and statute primarily upon the master, the servant has a high degree of responsibility for his own safety which, under the **Law Reform (Contributory**

Negligence) Act, 1945, he disregards at his peril. This Act enables the judge to apportion *liability according to fault*, and it is very frequently invoked. The judge assesses the employee's share of the blame as this or that percentage and deducts this proportion from the total estimated value of his compensation. Saying that a man has been 100 per cent contributorily negligent is another way of saying he has lost his case.

Fault

'Fault' refers more to the actual causes of the injury than to failure to comply with particular legal duties. The effect of this may be, as we have seen (p. 49), that if the real blame attaches to the employee, any previous breach of duty by management will be wholly or largely disregarded. We shall now consider in more detail what sort of behaviour on the employee's part is 'blameworthy', and to what extent.

The judges are not unaware of the stresses of industrial life. In Caswell v. Powell Duffryn, 1940, for instance, sympathetic account was taken of 'the long hours and the fatigue . . . the slackening of attention which naturally comes from constant repetition of the same operation . . . the noise and confusion in which a man works . . . his preoccupation in what he is actually doing, at the cost perhaps of some inattention to his own safety'. The conclusion was that 'it is not for every risky thing which a workman in a factory may do in his familiarity with machinery that he ought to be held guilty of contributory negligence'.

Motives

Wren v. Dixon, 1959, suggests that injuries incurred essentially through forwarding the employer's interests are unlikely to be affected by contributory negligence: Mr Justice Stable said there that 'the plaintiff is a highly responsible man, thoroughly competent and conscientious . . . In any case where I am quite satisfied that an injured man was not playing the fool, not indulging in some activity wholly outside his job, but perhaps through an excess of zeal takes what is really an unjustified risk or does so in a moment of absent mindedness or carelessness, I am loth to find that man is in any way in breach of his duty to his employer . . . He took a very considerable risk and was very foolish, but was actuated by one motive and one motive only – to further the interests of his employers. In all the circumstances I do not think there is room for a finding of contributory negligence against him.'

But these are very general observations and not by any means hard and fast rules. It is sometimes very difficult to assess the merits of behaviour by reference to motives rather than to what actually happened, or to distinguish good motives from bad. Dangerous working practices may be adopted not only because they are quicker ways of doing the employer's work, but also because they are easier and apparently more profitable for the employee. Accordingly the judges sometimes interpret devotion to duty as carelessness or disobedience, and penalize it accordingly, just as they may view the neglect of a moment as being as grave as prolonged indifference to personal safety. We shall see that it is virtually impossible to predict which view they will take in any given situation.

It is safe to say, however, that the employee will lose most or all of his damages if, for example, he habitually ignores clear safety rules, as in Woods v. Durable Suites (p. 48). If no express instructions were given, the employee is not necessarily in any stronger position. As we saw in many of the 'safe system' cases the danger may be so obvious and elementary that the employee's own common sense should suggest the precautions (McWilliams's case, p. 49). Pressure of work may be clearly established as a cause of such behaviour, but the outcome is not always very different. The judges say here, as they do in assessing employers' liability, that they distinguish between legal negligence and mere errors of judgment (Gallagher v. Dorman Long, 1947 – no contributory negligence by injured employee in estimating to the best of his ability what would be a safe load to lift). They have also said that they 'ought not to be too astute to find contributory negligence merely because the employee does not, every time he comes across a situation of extra hazard caused to him by his employer, refuse to work further' (Pead v. Furness Withy, 1965). Such comments should, however, be compared with some of other safe system cases mentioned in Chapter 2, such as Ashcroft v. Harden, Ross v. Associated Portland Cement, and Liffley v. Fairey Engineering. In all these a high degree of responsibility was put upon the employee to query the system under which he worked or to act with exceptional wisdom in emergency. Shilton v. Hughes Johnson, 1965, is another example. A millwright was injured when he put his head inside a drop hammer press to investigate a fault. He could have ordered the main power to be switched off, but did not do so because this would have stopped three other hammers and interfered with work accordingly. The judge said: 'I am sure he was doing his best for his employers', and reduced his damages by 60 per cent. In Simmons v. Bovis, 1956, the plaintiff was injured when 'without really having had time to direct his mind specifically to the sort of questions which he might have asked himself in other circumstances, he ducked under the guardrail and trod on this platform. The instinctive or semi-instinctive nature of the act also weighs with me'. His more or less instinctive act cost him 10 per cent of his claim. Where a man was injured because his tie caught in the unfenced machine he had to operate, he lost 50 per cent of the damages because he should have kept it tucked in his shirt and not his jacket; Lovelidge v. Odling, 1967.

Two remarkable cases, in which the only criticism of the employees was apparently that, in the words of Wrenn v. Dixon, above, they took 'an unjustified risk in a moment of carelessness . . . through an excess of zeal to further the interests of (their) employers', were Forgham v. Idoson, 1958, and Simmonds v. Walsall Conduits, 1962. In the first, a foundry foreman, described by the judge as 'assiduous and anxious to give a hand' was standing close to a mould which suddenly discharged molten metal over his feet. The employers were liable for the faulty mould, but the judge said that the foreman's 'momentary inadvertence and lack of the care which he should have observed played a major part in involving him in the injury', and so deprived him of half his compensation. In Simmonds's case, a foundry worker was burned when 'with extreme courage' he tried to prevent the flow of molten metal from a defective cupola. The county court judge found his employers negligent in providing wellington boots and not gaiters, but 'because of his frank statement that it was unlikely that he would have worn gaiters had they been available, he has failed to prove causation – that his employer's neglect to provide proper safety equipment was the cause of this accident'. The employee accordingly lost his claim entirely (*See* 'Burden of Proof', p. 101).

It may appear, therefore, that at least in claims for breach of common law duties, the law demands a standard of diligence from employees which is at least as high as that demanded from employers, and which it will relax only in the most exceptional cases.

Contributory Negligence in Breach of Statutory Duty Cases

A distinction must now be drawn between the effect of contributory negligence in common law claims such as those we have just considered, and its effect in claims for damages for breach of statutory duty. Since these duties are usually more specific than those of the common law and are enforceable by the strict terms of the criminal law, and since as we have seen (p. 70) they are intended to protect the careless as well as the careful worker, it is sometimes more difficult for the employer to escape liability.

In the familiar 'pressure of work' cases where employees deliberately lift or ignore guards in order to get on with the work, the employer may still bear some 50 per cent of the liability for the ensuing injury (Cross v. Segal, 1952; Smith v. Chesterfield Co-op, 1953; Biles v. Decca, 1960). The precise figure will depend very much on the obviousness of the risk, management's knowledge of the frequency or otherwise of the practice, and the effectiveness of supervision in preventing it. Even the most foolish or reckless conduct on the employee's part will not relieve the employer of all liability if he has failed to carry out his own obligations in the first place. In Maguire v. Fraser, 1966, an employee was injured when he deliberately or unnecessarily put his hand on to the cutters of an unfenced machine. The court none the less held the employer 20 per cent to blame. The judge said that where a person suffered an injury which fencing was intended to prevent, it must be 'rare in the extreme' that the absence of such fencing was not a cause of the accident. In Leech v. Standard Telephones, 1966, the plaintiff knew he had no business to use the machine, and ought to have known that his use of it was dangerous. The employer was accounted 25 per cent to blame for his initial failure to fence the machine. The same 75:25 division of liability took place in Clark v. Dartmouth Auto Castings, 1958, where an experienced fitter was injured when attempting to clear an obstruction from an unfenced machine which was in motion – an act whose 'extreme danger would have been obvious to a child'. Uddin v. Associated Portland Cement, 1965, and Allen v. Aeroplane Co., 1965, are other examples of misconduct by employees which still resulted in a nominal award against the employer.

In Rushton v. Turner Asbestos, 1959, it was held that despite the employer's original failure to guard the machine, 'the plaintiff was the sole author of his own misfortune', and so his claim was dismissed altogether. The more recent cases mentioned in the last paragraph, however, do not seem to favour this approach. The only circumstances in which a finding of 100 per cent contributory negligence against the employee may now be expected, are where the employer's breach of duty is purely 'technical', i.e. he has taken every conceivable precaution, and in the face of the clearest danger the employee removes the guard; or where the injury is wholly unpredictable; Manwaring v. Billington, 1952; Edwards v. McAlpine, 1952; Burns v. Terry, 1950. A final exceptional case which may conveniently be mentioned here arises where the worker is using the equipment in his own time and for his own private purposes (Napieralski v. Curtis, 1959 – employee not in course of employment – employer not liable for unfenced machine).

CONSENT

In the nineteenth century the judges tended to say that the servant's knowledge of danger in his work meant that he had agreed to run the risk of being injured, and so could not sue the master. They applied the maxim *volenti non fit injuria*, that is, 'if you consent, you can't complain'. This still holds good in many situations, e.g. for spectators at a cricket match. But it is now clearly established that *knowledge of the risk is not the same as voluntary acceptance of it so far as conditions of work are concerned.* Since the employee is not usually in a position to control these conditions it would be unjust in the extreme to deprive him of damages merely because he continues working where he knows there are hazards (Bill v. Short and Harland, 1962; D'Urso v. Sanson, 1939; Baker v. Jones, 1921 – knowledge respectively of compressed air pipes on factory floor, danger from sudden fire on employer's premises, and of defective brakes – no consent). In any case, consent cannot be raised as a defence to claims for breach of statutory duty; Wheeler v. New Merton Mills, 1933.

The defence is now rarely raised in master and servant cases, though it may operate as between principal and independent contractor where the duty of care is less stringent (*see* p. 99). Before an employer could defeat an employee's claim by this defence, he would have to prove not only his full understanding of the risk, but also his voluntary agreement to run it. This might be done by establishing that the risk is an obvious and inherent part of the job (though *see* Merrington v. Ironbridge Metal Works, 1952, as to the limits on the risks a fireman undertakes) or, for example, that the worker has accepted danger money.

Danger Money; Effect of Consent

Payment of danger money does not relieve management of taking all practicable precautions; it is intended only as a recognition that risks remain against which no precautions are practicable. Or the employer might prove consent by showing that the worker's method of doing the job defied the clearest instructions and created obvious and unnecessary risks, as in Shatwell's case (p. 55). If consent does operate as a defence it appears to defeat the employee's claim completely. But if the defence is rejected, the man's conduct in the face of a known risk may still amount to contributory negligence, and his damages would be reduced accordingly; Lovelidge v. Odling, p. 107. As this last point shows, consent and contributory negligence have different effects, so that, for example, consent may operate to defeat an employee's claim despite the fact that he has taken all possible care for his own safety.

Damages

GENERAL AND SPECIAL DAMAGES

If the injured employee is able to overcome all the obstacles set out above, and prove the employer's negligence or breach of statutory duty, then he is entitled to a sum of money called damages. Damages are classified as 'general', i.e. an estimate in financial terms of past and future loss of earnings, and 'special'. Special damages represent the known and precise loss to the date of the trial, notably loss of earnings and expenses. From the point of view of both medical treatment and legal rights it is most important to both sides that even trivial injuries should be promptly reported and recorded. This is in fact a legal obligation if industrial injuries benefit may be claimed. An accident book must be kept for this purpose in factories, mines, and business premises where there are more than ten employees.

Basis of Assessment

The purpose of an award of damages is to compensate the injured person for his injury; to put him back, in the limited ways in which money can achieve this, where he was before the accident. For this reason the judge's assessment of damages should take into account all relevant personal factors. Although no strict mathematical formula can be applied, nor will the calculation be itemized, the basis of the award is loss of earning capacity. This means that the judge must estimate what the plaintiff might have earned in the future, and how far he has been prevented from earning it. Any possibility of alternative lighter work will be taken into account and the award reduced accordingly. The judges deduct from the remaining sum an amount representing income tax which the plaintiff might have expected to pay on future earnings. A number of other factors are then taken into consideration which may substantially increase the award. These include pain, suffering, disfigurement, loss of marriage prospects, and loss of enjoyment of life such as inability to participate in sport or follow other personal interests. The nature of these losses is such that they could never be precisely expressed in money and so within broad limits the awards may vary considerably from case to case and judge to judge.

Expectation of life

A crucial point in all these calculations is that our judges will not attempt to forecast a man's situation for more than about fifteen years after the trial. They will not, in other words, allow to anyone an expectation of life of more than fifteen to eighteen years, even if the injury takes place in the late 'teens or early twenties. The expectation varies with age: for example, at 40 it is about twelve years; at 60, six or seven, and so on. These figures seem to have little or no actuarial basis. A recent illustration of some of the above points is in Price v. Crosse, 1966, where the plaintiff 'had his life wholly broken by appalling injuries' at the age of 17. The judge said: 'He was earning £5 13s. a week as a carpenter's apprentice. This is a case in which clearly the highest conventional multiplier should be applied, and I will assume the plaintiff's weekly net earnings as a qualified carpenter to be £15 a week over fifteen years . . . He has a small but extremely restricted place in the labour market, and I estimate his earnings capacity as £5 a week, so that the loss is £10 a week over fifteen years.' The total sum awarded was £17,500, i.e. including some £10,000 to compensate for pain and suffering.

A young man or woman with worse injuries and better prospects might receive substantially more, again because of the idea of individual compensation. So for example a management trainee of 21 who was completely paralysed in a road accident (where exactly the same considerations apply) received some £30,000 in another case in 1966. This is the average maximum award of recent years. Less serious injuries result in appropriately smaller awards. Thus: slinger, 37, loss of foot, alternative work – £5,000; foreman, 37, severe crush injury to right heel, ability to hold or find job affected – £850; scaffolder, 35, fractured ankle, had to give up football and dancing – £750; building worker, 61, fractured jaw, continuing noise in ear, sleep affected, some loss of hearing in one ear – £1,000; police constable, 41, loss of one eye, slight injury to other, disadvantageous position in labour market on retirement at 50 – £3,250.

If the injury is so grave as to make it reasonably certain that the plaintiff will not live even for the limited number of years normally contemplated by the judges, then the award is reduced accordingly. Thus in Baker v. Stanton, 1966, an apprentice joiner of 17 suffered an injury which caused quadriplegia (complete paralysis). The judges in the Court of Appeal said that if the plaintiff had then had a normal expectation of life the award would have been in the area of £30,000 or £35,000. Because of internal infection his expectation was reduced to perhaps ten years. He was awarded £25,000 general damages. This case and others such as West v. Shephard, 1963, and Naylor v. Yorkshire Electricity Board, below, lend support to the saying that 'it is cheaper to kill than to maim'.

Damages on Death

Where a person is killed as a result of an accident, in circumstances such that had he lived he would have had a claim against the other party, certain dependent relatives have a right to claim damages. The claim is based on their net financial loss – loss of the 'breadwinner' – and not any non-financial considerations such as grief or shock (Fatal Accidents Acts, 1846–1959). From this award is deducted any monetary benefit arising from the deceased's will or intestacy, other than money due under insurance policies or national insurance. If the plaintiff is a widow, the law's attempt to assess her loss usually requires the judge to estimate her attractiveness or otherwise so far as it may affect her prospects of remarriage. Thus Mr. Justice Waller: 'I have to take into account the possibility that the plaintiff, who, if she will forgive me saying so, is a very good-looking woman, might remarry, although as she has said, she has no intention of doing so' (Miller v. B.R.S. 1967). A claim may also be made on behalf of the deceased's estate, not only for loss of earnings but for other personal factors such as loss of expectation of life; Law Reform (Miscellaneous Provisions) Act, 1934. Claims under both Acts are usually brought by the same dependent relatives, and one award given under both headings. That part of the award attributed to the 1934 Act tends to be in hundreds rather than thousands of pounds; Naylor v. Yorkshire Electricity Board, 1967 – £500 for death of 20 year old. Claims under either Act must be brought within three years of the death.

Time limits

Claims for damages in non-fatal cases must be initiated within three years of the accident or occurrence of the disease, except that where a person suffers an injury or contracts a disease whose ill-effects may take more than three years to show themselves, he must then initiate proceedings within one year after they appear; Law Reform (Limitation of Actions) Act, 1953; Limitation Act, 1963. An exceptional thirty-year period is given for radiation injuries. If an injured person instructs his solicitor to issue a writ within the prescribed period, and the solicitor negligently fails to do so, or by other such delays nullifies the claim, the solicitor himself may be liable in damages; Yardley v. Coombes, 1963; Fitzgerald v. Batgers, 1967.

PROBLEMS

This brief outline may indicate some of the complications in awards of damages. The decision of the court, apart from any immediate appeal, is on a once and for all basis. No real attempt is made to ascertain the plaintiff's actual life span (contrary to the rule in Australia and New Zealand – two other common law countries – where damages may be awarded to cover, say, thirty years' loss of earnings). Deterioration or improvement in the plaintiff's condition cannot be taken into account except so far as can be estimated from medical evidence available at the trial. Further, the courts do not usually appear to recognize the continuing rapid decline in the value of money (though they acknowledged it in Miller's case, above), nor can they anticipate how earnings or taxation may fluctuate.

Costs; Legal Aid and Advice

Other difficulties which though not peculiar to personal injuries cases are often experienced in them are firstly, the very high cost of legal proceedings, and secondly, the delays. The legal aid and advice scheme extends to claims for damages for personal injuries, but the State will only pay all the costs if the plaintiff's disposal income (i.e. after deduction of taxes, rates, etc.) is less than £250 a year, or part of the cost if it is under £700. A proportion of any damages recovered may be taken by the State to repay the legal aid fund. For practical purposes it may be said that a family man earning more than about £1,500 gross could not claim legal aid, and so might face a bill of several hundred pounds if he lost a major case. Legal advice, however, may be obtained from most solicitors at a flat rate of £1 for half an hour's interview. Union support in making a claim is clearly desirable.

Delay

The problem of delay is equally serious, not only so far as accuracy of evidence is concerned, but also because of the adverse effect on the plaintiff's recovery, in mental, physical, and financial terms. In a case in 1966 Mr Justice Phillimore commented that a nine-year delay in bringing the case to trial 'reflects no credit on the legal profession'. In the same year Mr Justice Glyn Jones appealed for a 'sense of urgency' on the part of legal and other advisers when he heard a case which arose out of an accident in 1961. He said: 'In my experience it is becoming the rule rather than the exception for these actions to be brought four, five, six or even more years after the relevant accident. These delays militate against the rehabilitation and recovery of the injured and add gravely to anxiety and unhappiness.' In Fitzgerald v. Batgers, 1967, however, it was stated on a random sample basis that the average time between the accident and setting it down for trial in the High Court was two and a half years.

The causes of these delays are varied. Apart from the possible absence of a 'sense of urgency', there is the very real problem of the effect of the injuries. Because the award is on a once and for all basis both parties are particularly anxious to see how the injuries may develop so that an accurate assessment can be made. This difficulty could even now be met by a trial shortly after the accident to assess liability alone, and a second and minor hearing at a later date to settle the precise award. But this is hardly ever done, even in the most necessary cases; Hawkins v. New Mendip Engineering, 1966.

Compulsory Insurance?
A further point is the possibility that the employer may not have the money to pay damages awarded against him. Factory occupiers as such are now compelled to insure themselves against such claims, unless they come under the Nuclear Installations (Licensing and Insurance) Acts, 1959–65. When a proposal to introduce compulsory employers' insurance was debated, and rejected, by the House of Lords in 1959, figures were given showing that the great majority of awards were in fact paid immediately, and the remaining few were paid at least in part, or by instalments. But cases were also cited of small businesses which were under-insured or without any financial backing, so that the employee or his family were 'cheated out of what was due to them'. This may of course happen even where payment is by instalments, which may unavoidably be so small as to be almost pointless. In a case in 1967 a driver uninsured for passenger liability was ordered to pay £31,000 for 'appalling injuries' to his passenger – at the rate of £3 per week. This would take 200 years to pay off.

Periodic Payments?
These various difficulties have led to a number of suggestions for reform, some of which are mentioned above. Other possible developments are that the court might order payments to be made periodically, as is done in West Germany, and not as a lump sum. Such payments could then take more accurate account of changes in circumstances, actual life span, development of injuries, decline in the value of money, etc. The awards could be subject to review after several years. Compulsory insurance would be more clearly necessary if this proposal were adopted. Another possibility is that all industrial injuries should be regarded as the employer's fault unless he can prove to the contrary. This shift in the burden of proof would certainly enable more employees to win their claims. Rules of this kind have been adopted in various places, e.g. in the New Zealand Coal Mines Acts, 1925–47.

But even if any such developments occurred, the view would no doubt remain that anything resembling the present test of fault is little more than a barren exercise in legal logic which can never provide satisfactorily for each year's tens of thousands of industrial casualties.

Certainly as the system stands today, the presence or absence of fault may depend on fine points of evidence, or the chance availability or otherwise of witnesses, so that some victims receive a measure of compensation while others equally or still more seriously hurt get nothing. It may be thought that the principle of 'punishing' the blameworthy should be preserved, by making them pay damages. But here again there are difficulties. The law's standards of fault or retribution seem largely unrelated to moral standards. A persistently reckless driver may never cause an accident, whereas a most careful man may do by a single moment's inadvertence. Which is the more blameworthy? Again, the actual punishment does not relate to the degree of fault either, since damages depend on the age and income of the victim. And in any case the existence of compulsory insurance rules for drivers at least means that the wrongdoer himself does not in any significant sense foot the bill. The punishment aspect, in other words, is a matter for the criminal law only.

In 1965 Lord Chief Justice Parker said of the compensation problem as it affected road casualties – where the considerations are much the same as in industry – that there were 'innumerable instances' of people injured through no fault of their own who had failed to prove fault by the other driver. He concluded: 'The law and its administration in this field is out of date, lacking in certainty, unfair in its incidence, and capable of drastic improvement.' The same point was made somewhat more picturesquely a few years ago by the American judge, Mr Justice Frankfurter: 'To apply the concepts of "negligence" and "proximate cause" to the infinite complexities of modern industry is like catching butterflies without a net.'

Absolute Liability?

Perhaps the most widely supported solution is that of *'absolute liability'*, which means that compensation is paid without proof of fault and dependent only on cause and effect. Liability of this kind is already imposed for certain kinds of accident, as under the rules of vicarious liability, liability for damage done by nuclear installations, by civil aircraft, etc. The main argument for extending the rule to all industrial and/or road casualties is that since they are the inevitable results of social progress, the society which has benefited by that progress should also make comprehensive provision for the sufferers. A possible exception is that payments should not be made to those who are entirely to blame for their own injuries – though whether it is reasonable to penalize a family even on these grounds is debatable. Certainly technicalities and court hearings should be cut to the absolute minimum, otherwise the value of the compensation is greatly reduced by legal fees, etc.

Objections

Among the greatest objections to a general rule of absolute liability is the cost – though it is unquestionable that very large sums of money would be saved if these injury cases were no longer contested in the courts. An industrial scheme might be met either by compelling employers to be adequately insured – an expense likely to be between 3 and 4 per cent of the wages bill, which could justifiably be passed on to the consumer – or out of general taxation. The first method is illustrated by the various Workmen's Compensation Acts in America, Canada, Australasia, and elsewhere. The British Criminal Injuries Compensation Board, which pays compensation to victims of violent crime, shows that the second method is equally possible. The precise amounts of money involved are very difficult to assess, depending as they do upon agreement as to the proper level of compensation. Existing Workmen's Compensation awards do not purport to be on the same scale as damages might be; indeed American experience in particular shows that without continued pressure the levels of compensation here may, just as with damages, drop far behind current standards of living. (The legal complications of the American scheme are also said to result in the injured workman receiving on average only 45 cents out of every assessment dollar.) The benefits are usually standardized, determined partly by the type of injury – and not by pain, suffering, loss of amenity or the like – and partly by previous income. A typical provision is three-quarters of previous income, up to a maximum income of say, $5,000 or $6,000 a year.

Another possible objection to absolute liability is that it would weaken individual responsibility; but there is surely no proof that the existing compulsory insurance makes drivers any the less careful for their own or others' safety. The only effective weapon here is in fact the criminal law. The final problem is – who should be protected under the proposed scheme? Would not the present arbitrary differences in treatment be just as great if industrial and road victims alone were singled out for automatic compensation? Perhaps, but the real choice seems to be between singling out areas of special risk and making adequate provision for them, or doing nothing.

Industrial Injuries Insurance Benefits

NATIONAL INSURANCE ACTS

Apart from the claim for damages, with all its expense and uncertainty, the injured employee may be entitled to industrial injuries insurance benefit. This benefit was introduced by the National Insurance (Industrial Injuries) Act, 1946, to replace the old Workmen's Compensation scheme. The principal Act is now that of 1965, as amended by the National Insurance Acts, 1966 and 1967. Industrial injuries benefit is different from an award of damages in various fundamental respects, chiefly in that the payment does not depend on proof of fault, and that it is not intended to compensate but only to provide a subsistence level. For the latter reason it is not in its present form a satisfactory alternative to an award of damages.

The insurance benefits are paid from a fund to which both employer and employee must, except for certain casual or 'inconsiderable' or family employment, contribute. The employer pays for national insurance stamps, which also provide for sickness, unemployment, etc., benefits, and deducts the employee's contribution to the stamp from his wages. For the adult employee the employer now pays 41*s*. a week, including the selective employment tax. The employee pays 15*s*. 8*d*. There is no minimum number of contributions which have to be made before benefit can be claimed, though the rule is different for unemployment and sickness. *So far as injury benefit is concerned, only those employed under a contract of employment or apprenticeship* (*see* p. 3) *are entitled to claim.* The benefits are set out below.

ENTITLEMENT TO BENEFIT

An employee has a right to injury benefit in two circumstances. The first is **where the injury is caused by an accident arising out of and in the course of employment.** If, in other words, the employee can show he was injured at work and because of the work, then he need not also prove negligence or breach of statutory duty by his employer. It is presumed on the claimant's behalf that injuries occurring at work arise out of that work. But that presumption may be displaced if, for example, the employee's activities at the time of the injury were completely unrelated to his work, even though within works time. To that extent only, his contributory negligence may be a bar to his claim. For example, where an employee is injured through disobedience, his claim depends on the extent to which he could still be said to have been carrying out his duties. If he is injured when leaving work by an unauthorized route, he would probably still be regarded as in the course of employment, whereas if he leaves by that route *before the proper time*, he would probably not be.

Incidental acts. Activities incidental to one's work, such as the meal break, or a visit to the toilet, or a pause for a cup of tea or a permitted cigarette, or for a word with another employee, are usually within the course of employment. Unjustified extensions of these rights are a different matter. Where a man sustained injury during a conversation which recklessly interfered with dangerous work, he was debarred from benefit. Again, 'where a man overstays a meal break disobediently, carelessly or negligently, that does not automatically take the man outside the course of his employment. It only does so when he is doing something different from what he is employed to do . . . In this case the claimant's accident did not arise in the course of his employment, in that he extended a tea break so as to make it last half as long again, which could not fairly be regarded as a reasonable incident of the employment' (R. v. Industrial Injuries Commissioner, *ex parte* A.E.U., 1965). Injuries caused by fellow-employees' or others' deliberate misconduct or practical joking are within employment and benefit will be paid, so long as the claimant's behaviour did not contribute to his injury.

Travel to and from work. There are contradictory decisions on the question of benefit for injuries sustained when travelling to or from work. Generally, employment only begins when the place of work is reached but this may be extended for those whose duty involves travel, e.g. to visit customers or attend meetings, and for those who are travelling in their employers' vehicles. Apart from such cases of express or implied authority to travel by that method or route or at that time, it is difficult to regard injuries which anyone using a public highway is exposed to as sustained in the course of employment. The problems are similar to those involved in the doctrine of vicarious liability (p. 54), though as a rule 'course of employment' is more generously interpreted for purposes of insurance benefit.

Injury benefit is payable, as stated above, for 'accidents' at work. This word excludes disabilities which cannot be traced to particular moments in time, or where there is no sufficiently specific cause and effect. Thus a gradual deterioration in health during years of work in damp or other such conditions will not be regarded as an accident for the purposes of the Act.

Prescribed Diseases

The second ground on which an employee may claim industrial injury insurance benefit is where he has suffered **any prescribed disease or personal injury not caused by accident but due to the nature of the employment.** Under this rule a large number of 'occupational hazards' have been identified, and there is usually a presumption that the disease has been contracted because of the work. The prescribed diseases include, for example, lead poisoning resulting from any use or handling of or exposure to lead fumes, dust or vapour; tuberculosis from work in hospitals or on medical research; heat cataracts from exposure to molten or red hot material; dermatitis caused by work which exposes the employee to dust, liquid, vapour or other course of skin irritation including friction or heat; and pneumoconiosis or other similar lung diseases caused by mining, foundry, pottery or other occupations involving exposure to dust. If a person who is not in one of the specified occupations contracts a prescribed disease, he may still receive insurance payments if he can show it arose by accident in the course of his employment, as above.

BASIC BENEFITS

Injury Benefit

The benefits in non-fatal cases are of two kinds, basic and additional. The basic award may be either *injury* benefit or *disablement* benefit. Injury benefit is payable for the first six months of incapacity for work. There is no incapacity if different or lighter work could reasonably be undertaken. Payment will not be made for isolated days' absence from work. There must be two or more days' incapacity within six consecutive days. Nor is payment made for the first three days of incapacity, unless followed by at least nine further days within thirteen weeks of the first day, or unless there has been a previous spell of incapacity within the preceding thirteen weeks. The amount of the basic injury benefit varies according to which of four age groups the claimant is in. The groups are; men or women over 18, young persons between 17 and 18, boys and girls under 17 but over school-leaving age or in full-time employment, and boys and girls under school-leaving age in part-time employment. The weekly rate for men and women over 18 is (1967) £7 5s. 0d.

Disablement Benefit

The second kind of basic award, disablement benefit, is usually payable at the end of the injury benefit period. But it may be given immediately after the accident occurs, if the resulting disability is not such as to cause incapacity for work. The amount of the award in either case depends on the nature of the disability, as laid down in the Benefit Regulations, 1964, and/or as assessed by a medical board. Assessment is on a percentage basis, with a minimum requirement of loss of physical or mental capacity over 1 per cent, as compared with a normal person of the same age and sex. Loss of wages as such does not affect the assessment (so that as mentioned above disability payment may still be made though the employee remains at work). A disability assessed at 100 per cent, such as loss of sight or of both hands or feet, represents a pension of £7 12s. 0d. a week; 50 per cent disabilities include loss of four fingers on one hand; 40 per cent, loss of one eye; 30 per cent, one thumb, and so on. If the disability is less than 20 per cent (£1 10s. 6d. a week), a lump sum is normally paid. The maximum 'gratuity' for a 19 per cent disability is £500, based on a seven-year pension, but this may be reduced according to the nature of the injury. Any assessment may be increased if the employee's previous state of health subjects him to a greater disability than would normally be suffered, as where a hand injury follows a previous injury to the other hand, or reduced if medical evidence shows that his condition was such as to make the particular injury or its effect inevitable (e.g. previous mental instability which after a comparatively trivial injury results in extreme neurotic symptoms).

Additional Benefits

Injury benefits can be increased by allowances for dependent relatives and by earnings-related sickness benefit (*see* below), and disablement benefits by these and other allowances. The weekly rate for adult dependants is £2 16s. 0d. A disablement pension may be added to by a special hardship allowance, where the injury causes a continuing reduction in earning power as compared with the claimant's previous regular occupation, or by an unemployability supplement for permanent unfitness for work (but disregarding earnings up to £104 p.a.), and by constant attendance and hospital treatment allowances. The amounts vary, the largest being £9 a week where constant attendance upon an exceptionally severely disabled person is necessary. Sickness benefit can also be paid if the employee is unable to work after the twenty-six weeks of his injury benefit period, but not if he receives the unemployability supplement. By the National Insurance Act, 1966, sickness benefit rates are related to earnings, so that an additional sum of not more than £7 a week (i.e. one-third of earnings between £9 and £30) is payable for six months after the twelfth day of incapacity. In no case may the benefits exceed 85 per cent of the employee's weekly earnings.

Disqualification

A claim for insurance benefit may be disqualified for up to six weeks if the employee refuses to follow medical treatment or to submit to a necessary medical examination or undergo a prescribed training or rehabilitation course. Claims must usually be made within six days of the incapacity (twenty-one days for the first claim), and benefit will not be paid for any period more than six months before the date of claim.

Death Benefit

The widow of an employee killed as a result of an accident at work or through a prescribed industrial disease is entitled to a pension of £6 7s. 0d. a week for twenty-six weeks. This may be supplemented by not more than £7 a week under the National Insurance Act, 1966, as above. The allowance is reduced after the first six months to £5 10s. 0d. or £1 10s. 0d. according to the widow's circumstances. Further sums up to £2 2s. 6d. a week may be claimed for a dependent child. If the widow remarries, her pension ceases but she receives a gratuity equal

DEFENCES, DAMAGES, AND INSURANCE

to one year's pension. After remarriage her child allowances continue, but at a reduced rate. Parents and other dependent relatives may also be entitled to small pensions or lump sums if they have been partly or wholly maintained by the deceased employee.

Claims

Claims for disablement benefit are made to a medical board, and thence to a medical appeal tribunal. Other claims for industrial injuries benefits are made first to an insurance officer, with a right of appeal to an insurance tribunal, and thence to the Industrial Injuries Insurance Commissioner. Questions of law may be considered on appeal to the High Court. An important distinction between insurance benefits and damages is that the former depend on the injured person's state of health, and may be increased or reduced accordingly.

Damages and Insurance Payments

It should be noted finally that injured employees will be entitled to both insurance benefit and damages if they can prove that their injuries occurred at work *and* were caused by their employer's fault. Where these two rights arise, the Law Reform (Personal Injuries) Act, 1948, in effect deducts the value of the employer's stamp contributions from the damages. The Act provides that one-half of the insurance benefits which might accrue to the injured man within not more than five years following his injury shall be deducted from that part of the damages which represents future loss of earnings.

*

One final word – it pays to keep clear of the law!

Index

Abrasive wheels, 61
Abstract of Factories Act, 91
Access 36–8, 63, 73–5, 102
Accident book, 110
Accident rate, 75, 86
Accidents: *See* Employer's Liabilities; Factories Act; Industrial Injuries Insurance; Notification of Accidents
Act of God, 102
Administrative and clerical work, 63–4
Advice, 56
Aerated water, 60, 82
Agriculture (Safety, Health, and Welfare Provisions) Act, 59
Alternative employment, 27
Ambulance room, 81
Animals, slaughter, 63
Annual returns, 92
Anthrax, 61
Apprentices, 6, 10
Arrest, 56
Asbestos, 60, 82, 85
Assault, 43, 56

Ballot, 88
Barrier cream, 40, 82
Biscuit factories, 79
Blast furnaces, 81
Blasting of castings, 60
Boilers and receivers, 76
Boots and spats: *See* Safety Equipment
Brass casting, 65
Breach of contract, 9, 12–22, 24, 52
Breathing apparatus, 75, 76
   See also Respirators
Bronzing, 60, 82
Building and Construction, 4, 34, 49–51, 60, 73, 75, 78, 81–3, 90, 93
Bullying, 43
Burden of proof, 40, 61, 83, 101, 107
Business connections, 12

Canteens 38, 45, 54, 63, 75, 81
Care
   by employee
      standards of work, 15, 27
      safety duties, 54–5, 92–3
      See also Contributory Negligence
   by employer
      See Employer's Liabilities; Factories Act; Regulations for Dangerous Trades
Cases cited, 2
Celluloid and cellulose solutions, 60, 77, 85–6
Cement works, 81–2, 84
Checkweighing in Various Industries Act, 91, 93
Chemical works, 60, 76–7, 79, 81, 83–5, 93
Cheque, payment by, 7
Children, as Trespassers, 99
Chromium plating, 60, 66, 79, 82
Cinematograph film, 60
Civil law, definition, 1
   See also Employer's Liabilities; Factories Act; Damages.
Clay works, 81
Cleaning of machinery, 72

Cleanliness, 38, 64, 66–7, 92
Cloakrooms, 63, 80
Clothing: *See* Protective Clothing; Safety Equipment
Clothing accommodation, 80
Coal Mines Acts (New Zealand), 115
Collective agreements, 8, 10, 25
Collective disobedience, 55
Common employment, 52
Common law, definition, 1
   See also Contract of Employment, implied terms; Employer's Liabilities
Companies Act, 4
Competence, 14, 15, 27
'Competent person', 43, 76
Competition from employees, 12, 17
Complaints, 14, 37, 43, 91
Compressed air, work in, 60, 65, 78–9, 81, 90, 92–3
Confined spaces, work in, 46, 75–6
Consent, 55, 98–9, 109–10
Conspiracy and Protection of Property Act, 21
Construction: *See* Building and Construction
Continuity of employment, 23–4, 28
Continuous daily employment, 87
Contract of employment, 1–31, 52–7, 118
   breach, 9, 12–22, 24, 52
   changes in terms, 8–9
   course of employment distinguished, 53–7
   definition, 3–6, 118
   express terms, 9, 49, 52–6
   form, 6–8
   implied terms, 9–19
   impossibility, 22
   notice, 22–5
   parties, 2–6
   signatures, 9
   termination, 18–30
   See also Contracts of Employment Act; Redundancy Payments Act; Industrial Injuries Insurance; Holidays; Sickness
Contracts of Employment Act, 2, 6–9, 21, 23–5
   apprentices, 6
   changes in terms, 8, 9
   continuity of employment, 23–4, 28
   employees excluded, 8, 23
   notice, 23–5
   part-time employees, 8, 23
   payment, 11
   strikes, 24
   summary dismissal, 24
   written statement, 7–9
Contributory negligence, 17, 35, 38, 45, 47–8, 50, 70, 73, 92–3, 95, 98, 100, 104, 110, 119
Control, test of, 3–6
Cost of legal proceedings, 114
Cost of safety precautions, 35, 36
Cotton processes, 60, 65, 84–5
Course of employment
   employer's liabilities for employees' wrongful acts, 53–7
   employer's liabilities to employees, 109
   industrial injuries insurance, 118–20, 123
Cranes, 73, 86

124

INDUSTRIAL LAW

Criminal Injuries Compensation Board, 117
Criminal law, 1
  See also Criminal Negligence: Factories Act
Criminal negligence, 33

Damages
  breach of contract, 9–13
  breach of safety duties, 10, 32, 57, 61, 64, 101, 110–18, 123
  See also Contributory Negligence
Danger money, 110
Dangerous occurrences: See Notification of Accidents
Dangerous trades: See Regulations for Dangerous Trades; Chemical Works; Power Presses; Potteries
Death benefit, 122–3
Defamation, 12, 21
Defences, employer's, 101–110
Delays in legal proceedings, 114–15
Delegation, 36, 51, 57, 103–4
Dependents, 112–13, 122–3
Dermatitis, 39–40, 48, 120
Deviation from route, 55
Disablement benefit, 121–3
Dismissal
  with notice, or money in lieu, 7, 11, 15, 19, 22–7
  without notice, 9, 13, 15–19, 24, 26–7, 29, 50
  wrongful, 13, 19, 21, 26
  See also Contracts of Employment Act; Redundancy Payments Act
Diving operations, 60
Docks, 37, 60, 85, 90
Dock Workers Order, 10, 23, 25
Doctor, 86
  See also Factory Doctor; Medical Board; Medical Examination
Drainage, 66
Drinking water, 79
Dry cleaning, 60
Dust, 48, 50, 76, 80, 82–3, 86, 120
Dyeing, 79, 82

Electricity, 60, 71, 75, 82, 86
Electric accumulators, 60, 65, 90
Employee
  breach of contract, 19–21, 52
  claims for damages by breach of contract, 21–2
  injury, 11, 32–6, 59, 61, 95, 101–10, 123
  See also Employer's Liabilities; Factories Act; Damages
  contractual rights and duties, 8–19
  definition, 3–6
  dismissal, 5, 9, 13–31
  disabled, 2, 35, 45
  duties under Factories Act, 82, 92–3
  industrial injuries insurance, 118–23
  redundancy payments, 25–30
  unemployment insurance, 30–1
  See also Holidays; Pay; Women and Young Persons
Employer
  breach of contract, 21–2
  claims for damages by, 9, 13, 19–20, 52
  contractual rights and duties, 2–3, 8–18
  definition, 3–6
  defences, 101–10
  national insurance payments, 118, 123
  insurance, 5, 115
  references and testimonials, 12–13
  trade secrets and business connections, 11–12
  See also Employer's Liabilities; Factories Act; Damages

Employer's common law liabilities, 10, 32–58
  equipment, plant and machinery, 39–42, 69
  means of access, 37–8
  personal responsibility, 36, 41, 43, 51, 57
  premises, 36–9, 74
  reasonable care, 32–6, 53
  supervision and training, 42–3
  system of work, 44–52, 85, 106
Employer's liabilities for employees' wrongful acts, 51–8, 97, 102
  contract, 56–7
  course of employment, 53–7, 120
  crime, 57
  tort, 53–6
Employer's liabilities for independent contractors, 57–8
Employment
  contract and conditions: See Contract of Employment
  course of employment, 53–7, 109, 118–20, 123
  definition, 3–6
  general and particular, 5, 97
  part-time, 8, 23–4, 29
  termination, 18–30
Employment of Women, Young Persons and Children Act, 89
Enamelling, 60, 65, 79, 82
Equipment, plant and machinery, safety of, at common law, 39–42
  See also Factories Act; Owner's Liability for Equipment
Explosions, 86
Express terms, 9, 49, 52–6
Eye protection, 60
  See also Goggles

Factories Act, 1, 5, 32, 43, 57, 59–96
  access, 73–5, 102
  abstract and other notices, 91–2
  ambulance rooms, 81
  bakehouses, 84, 96
  ballot, 88
  breathing apparatus, 75–6
  boilers and receivers, 76
  checkweighing, 93
  civil and criminal proceedings, 57, 61, 94–6
  cleanliness, 64, 66
  clothing accommodation, 80
  common law, compared, 1, 59, 61
  'competent person', 43, 76
  confined spaces, 75–6
  cranes, 73, 86
  definition and extensions, 61–3, 90, 96
  doctor, 87–90, 92, 94
  drainage, 66
  dust, 76, 82
  employee's duties, 82, 92–3
  exemptions, 64, 66, 88–90
  fencing of machinery, 57, 67–72, 92, 102, 104, 108–9
  fines, 57, 61, 94–6
  fire precautions, 76–7, 86, 92, 94
  first aid, 80–1
  floors and passageways, 63–5, 73–5, 102
  fumes, 65, 75–6, 82
  goggles and screens, 83–4
  health sections, 64–7, 82–5
  home work, 90–1
  hours of work, 87–9, 92
  humidity, 84, 96
  independent contractors, 67, 75
  inspectors, 61, 64–6, 77–9, 84–95
  ladders, 74–5
  laundries, 63, 65, 81–2, 84, 87, 89, 91
  lifts and lifting equipment, 73, 77, 86
  lighting, 65–7
  'machinery attendants', 71–2

125

INDEX

Factories Act–*continued*
  manual labour, 61–3
  meals, 80–1, 83, 87–8
  medical examination and supervision, 66, 81, 88–90, 92
  noise, 66
  notification of accidents and dangerous occurrences, 85–6, 92
  obstructions, 74–6
  occupier, 61, 90, 94–6
  overtime, 87–8
  owner, 61, 90
  piece work, 91
  pits, tanks, vats, etc., 75–6
  poisonous substances, 83–6, 90, 92
  processes within the Act, 61–3
  prohibited processes and substances, 78–9
  protective clothing, 71, 81–2, 93
  register, 92
  regulations for dangerous trades, 1, 59–61 *See also:* Chemical Works; Power Presses; Woodworking Machinery
  rest and rest rooms, 81, 83, 87–8
  safety sections, 67–79, 82–5
  safety supervisors, 77–8
  sale or hire of machinery, 72
  seats, 80
  shift work, 87–8
  stairways, 63, 74
  temperature, 65
  toilets, 66
  underground rooms, 84
  ventilation, 65
  wages, 91
  water, 79
  weights, 45, 84–5
  welfare sections, 79–85
  women and young persons, 72, 84–5, 87–9, 92, 96
Factories inspectors, 41, 42, 49, 61, 64–6, 77–9, 84–95
Factory and Workshop Act, 96
Factory, definition, 61–3, 90, 96
Factory doctor, 87, 90, 92, 94
Factory notices, 91
Factory occupier, 61, 90, 94–6
Factory owner, 61, 90
Factory processes, 61–3
Factory register, 87, 92, 94
Fair wages resolution, 91
Farms, 59, 63
Fatal Accidents Acts, 112–13
Felt hats, 60
Fencing of machinery, 57, 67–72, 92, 102, 104, 108–9
File cutting, 60
Film production, 63
Fines
  by employer, 7
  by magistrates' court, 57, 61, 94–6
Fire and fire precautions, 76–7, 86, 92, 94
First aid, 80–1
Flax and tow, 60, 65
Floors and passageways, 36–8, 63–5, 73–5, 102
Foundries, 48–9, 60, 66, 75, 79, 81, 83–4, 88, 91, 101, 107, 120
Fruit preserving, 82
Fumes, 65, 75–6, 82, 120

Garages, 63
Gasholders, 63, 66
General and particular employment, 5, 97
General trade practice, 40
Glass processes, 81–2, 85
Gloves: *See* Safety Equipment
Goggles and screens, 35, 40, 45, 51, 81, 83, 101

Good faith, 16
Go-slow, 13
Grinding and grindstones, 46, 60, 65, 69, 70, 83, 93
Gut scraping, 82

Health Sections of Factories Act, 64–7, 82–5
Helmets: *See* Safety Equipment
Hemp and jute, 60
Hidden defects in equipment, 40
Hides and skins, 60
Hired-out labour, 5, 96–100
Hoists, 73, 77, 86
Holidays and holiday pay, 7, 11, 24, 88–9
Home work, 90
Honesty, 16, 17, 54
Horizontal milling machines, 60
Horsehair, 60
Hours of work, 87–9, 92
Humidity, 84, 96

Immigrant labour, 49
Implied terms of contract, 9–19
Incidental acts, 54, 119
Indemnity, 11, 15
Independent contractors, 3–5, 41, 57, 67, 75, 96–100
Indiarubber, 60, 65, 79, 90
Industrial Court, 10
Industrial injuries insurance, 86, 110, 118–23
  accidents arising out of and in course of employment, 118–20
  death benefit, 122–3
  disablement benefit, 121–3
  injury benefit, 120–2
  prescribed diseases, 120
Industrial Training Act, 3, 29, 42
Industrial tribunals, 8, 19, 29
Injunction, 20
Injuries at work: *See* Employer's Liabilities; Factories Act; Damages; Industrial Injuries Insurance
Injury benefit, 120–2
Inspection of equipment and machinery, 39, 46, 71–2, 76
Inspectors: *See* Factories Inspectors
Insurance, employer's, 5, 15, 115–18
Interviews, 17
Inventions, 18
Ionizing radiations, 60–1, 72, 78, 90, 92, 113
  See also Nuclear Installations (Licensing and Insurance) Acts

Journeys to and from work
  course of employment, 54, 119–20
  Redundancy Payments Act, 27
Jute, 60, 65, 71, 82, 85

Kiers, 60

Labour Exchange, 30
Laundries, 63, 65, 81–2, 87, 89, 91
Law Reform (Contributory Negligence) Act, 104–5
  See also Contributory Negligence
Law Reform (Limitation of Actions) Act, 113
Law Reform (Miscellaneous Provisions) Act, 113
Law Reform (Personal Injuries) Act, 43, 52, 123
  See also Employer's Liabilities for Employees' Wrongful Acts
Lay-off, 26
Lead processes, 60, 64, 79, 81–3, 85, 90–2
Legal aid and advice, 114
Lifting injuries, 45–6, 84–5, 106
Lifts and lifting equipment, 73, 77, 86
Lighting, 65–7

126

INDUSTRIAL LAW

Limitation Act, 113
Liquids, dangerous, 61, 72
Local authority, 62–4, 66, 90, 94, 96
Locomotives and wagons, 60
Luminizing, 60, 78, 80, 82, 90

'Machinery attendants', 71–2
Machinery: *See* Fencing of Machinery; Power Presses; Woodworking Machinery
Magistrates' court, 78, 94–5
Magnesium, 60, 82
Manual labour, definition, 61–2
Manufacturers' liability, 40, 72
Masks: *See* Respirators
Meals, 80–1, 83, 87–8, 119
Medical board and appeal tribunal, 123
Medical examination and supervision, 66, 81, 88–90, 92
Mines and Quarries Act, 32, 59–96, 104
 definition, 63
 management qualifications, 43, 78
 safety, representatives, 77–8, 85
 search, 7
 See also Access; Fencing of Machinery; Fire Precautions
Ministry of Labour, 1, 30, 59–60, 66, 77–8, 81, 83, 85–9, 91, 93, 96
Misconduct, 11, 13–19, 24, 27, 29, 119
 See also Contributory Negligence; Practical Jokes

National Insurance Acts, 2, 30–1, 118–23
 See also Industrial Injuries Insurance; Unemployment Insurance
Negligence: *See* Contributory Negligence; Reasonable Care
Noise, 66
Notice: *See* Dismissal; Contracts of Employment Act; Redundancy Payments Act
Notification of accidents and dangerous occurrences, 85–6, 92
Nuclear Installations (Licensing And Insurance) Acts, 115

Obedience, 9, 13–14, 27, 50, 54–5, 106, 119
Obstructions, 37–8, 74–6
Occupier, factory: *See* Factory Occupier
Occupiers' Liability Act, 32, 39, 58, 96–9
Offices, Shops, and Railway Premises Act, 59–96
 See also Cleanliness; Fencing of Machinery; Overcrowding
Oil cake mills, 81–2
Orders: *See* Obedience
Overcrowding, 64–6
Overtime, 7, 28, 87–8
Owner, factory: *See* Factory Owner
Owner's liability for equipment, 96, 99–100

Painting of factory, 64
Paints and painting, 60, 83, 90, 92
Parties to the contract of employment, definition, 2–6
Part-time employment, 8, 23–4, 29
Passageways: *See* Floors and Passageways
Patent fuel, 60, 80, 82, 84, 90
Patents Act, 18
Pay, 7, 10, 11, 21, 23, 26–8, 30, 54, 89, 91, 93
Payment of Wages Act, 7
Permitted acts, 56, 119
Phosphorus, 84–5
Photographic materials, 66
Piece work, 9, 28, 47–8, 91
Plant: *See* Equipment
Poisonous substances, 41, 83–6, 90, 92, 120
Potteries, 60, 64–6, 78–83, 85, 90, 120
Power presses, 1, 60, 71–2

Practical jokes, 42–3, 52, 119
Premises, safety of, at common law, 36–9
 See also. Factories Act; Occupiers' Liability Act
Prescribed diseases, 120, 122
Prices and Incomes Acts, 21
Printing and bookbinding, 63
Protective clothing, 71, 80–2, 93
 See also: Goggles; Safety Equipment

Reasonable care
 employer's personal duty at common law, 10–11, 32–51, 59, 69, 74, 82, 84–5
 employer's liability for employees' wrongful acts, 51–3
Factories Act, 69–70, 102
Receivers: *See* Boilers and Receivers
Redundancy Payments Act, 3, 19, 21, 24–30
 alternative employment, 27
 continuity of employment, 24, 28
 counter notice, 27
 definition of redundancy, 26–7
 dismissal, 26–7
 employees excluded, 29
 industrial tribunals, 29
 lay-off, 26–7
 notice of intention to claim, 26–7
 overtime, 28
 part-time employees, 29
 payments, 28
 redundancy fund and rebates, 29–30
 short-time, 26–7
 week's pay, 28
 written requirements, 26–9
References and testimonials, 12
Refractory materials, 60
Register: *See* Factory Register
Regulations for dangerous trades, 1, 59–61, 85, 96
 See also Chemical Works; Power Presses; Woodworking Machinery
Reinstatement, 22, 25
Remoteness of damage, 34, 102–3
Research, 41–2, 63, 96
Respirators, 48, 81–3
Restraint of trade, 11–12, 20
Restrictive Practices Court, 12
Rest and rest-rooms, 81, 83, 87–8
Road vehicle lifting machines, 60
Ropes and chains, 73

Safety campaigns, 48–9, 96
Safety councils, 77–8
Safety duties, employer's: *See* Employer's Liabilities; Factories Act
Safety equipment
 belts, 37, 50–1, 82
 boots and spats, 49, 61, 107
 gloves, 81–2
 helmets, 81
 See also Goggles; Protective Clothing; Respirators
Safety leaflets, 92
Safety officer, 40, 77
Safety rules, common law, general, 50–1
Safety Sections of Factories Act, 67–79, 82–5
Safety supervisor, 77–8, 104
Sale and hire of machinery, 72
Salt processes, 85
Saw mills, 81
Screens: *See* Goggles and Screens
Seamen, 35, 59
Search, 7
Seats, 80–1
Secrets, 11
Selective employment tax, 3, 4, 118
Self-acting machinery, 72

127

INDEX

Self-employment: See Independent Contractors
Shift work, 28, 87–8
Shipbuilding and repairing, 60, 63, 75, 78, 81–4, 90–2
Shops, 89, 98
Shops Act, 89
    See also Offices, Shops, and Railway Premises Act
Shop steward, 39, 92
Short-time, 24, 26
Sickness and sick pay, 7, 11, 14–15, 24, 31, 118
Spare-time activities, 17–18
Solicitors, 113–14
Spinning mules, 60, 90
Stairways, 38, 63, 74–5
Statute law, definition, 1
Statutory instruments: See Regulations for Dangerous Trades; Chemical Works; Power Presses; Woodworking Machinery
Students, 63
Sugar factories, 81
Suggestion schemes, 18
Suitable alternative employment: See Alternative Employment
Supervisor's responsibilities, 3, 10, 34, 36, 39, 42, 44, 47, 49–51, 72, 108
Suspension, 7
Sweet factories, 91
System of work, safety of, at common law, 44–52, 85, 106

Tanning, 79, 82
Technical colleges, 63
Temperature, 64–6
Terms of Conditions of Employment Act, 10, 91
Terms of contract of employment: See Contract of Employment
Testing of aircraft engines, 60, 66, 93
Testing of equipment, 41–2, 63
    See also Power Presses; Lifts and Lifting Equipment
Theft, 80
Time limits for bringing claims
    damages, 113
    industrial injuries insurance, 122
    redundancy payment, 29
Time worker, 29
Tinning, 60, 82, 90
Toilets, 38, 64, 66–7, 75
Tool setters, 47, 71

Trade Disputes Acts, 20
Trade unions, 1, 4, 8, 13–14, 16, 20–1, 25, 37, 86, 94, 114
    See also Collective Agreements; Shop Steward
Travel: See Journeys to and from work
Trespassers, 99
Truck Acts, 7

Underground rooms, 84
Unemployment insurance, 28, 30–1, 118
Unfenced machinery, 71, 92
    See also Fencing of Machinery

Ventilation, 64–5, 67, 82, 101
Vicarious liability: See Employer's Liability for Employees' Wrongful Acts
Visitors, 96–100

Wages: See Pay; Wages Councils
Wages Councils: Wages Councils Act, 10, 11, 89
Washing facilities, 79
Weights: See Lifting Injuries
Welding, 83–4
    See also Goggles
Welfare Sections of Factories Act, 79–85
Women and young persons, 72, 84, 85, 87–90, 92, 96
Woodworking machinery, 60, 65, 69–72, 75
Woollen processes, 60, 64–5, 79, 81, 83, 85, 91, 93
Work, duty to provide, 10
Workers' Protection Act (Sweden), 78
Workplace safety of: See Employer's Common Law Liabilities; Factories Act
Works' rules books, 6, 8, 48–9
Work-to-rule, 13
Written terms of contract, 6–9, 16–18, 23, 48–9
    See also Redundancy Payments Act
Wrongful dismissal: See Dismissal

Yarn, 60, 79, 83, 90
Young persons, common law duty to supervise, 42
    See also Women and Young Persons

Zeal, 55
Zinc, 85